Beyond
the
Ivy Wall

Also by Howard Greene and Robert Minton:

Scaling the Ivy Wall:
12 Winning Steps to College Admission

Beyond the Ivy Wall

10 Essential Steps to Graduate School Admission

HOWARD GREENE and
ROBERT MINTON

LITTLE, BROWN AND COMPANY
BOSTON   TORONTO   LONDON

FIRST EDITION

Library of Congress Cataloging-in-Publication Data

Greene, Howard, 1937–
    Beyond the ivy wall: 10 essential steps to graduate school admission / by Howard Greene, and Robert Minton. — 1st ed.
        p.   cm.
    Bibliography: p.
    Includes index.
    ISBN 0-316-32684-4
    1. Universities and colleges — United States — Graduate work — Admission.   2. Professional education — United States — Admission. 3. Universities and colleges — United States — Graduate work — Finance. 4. Professional education — United States — Finance.   I. Minton, Robert, 1918–   . II. Title.
LB2371.4.G74 1989   89-31792
378.1'056 — dc20.   CIP

10 9 8 7 6 5 4 3 2

RRD-VA

Published simultaneously in Canada
by Little, Brown & Company (Canada) Limited

PRINTED IN THE UNITED STATES OF AMERICA

Contents

Admissions Decisions · Selecting Programs for Your Talents · Assuring Your MBA Admission · What Admissions Offices Say · Who Gets In? · Innovative Management Programs · MEDICAL SCHOOL. Admission Is Still a Challenge · Six Preparatory Procedures · Study Medical School Admissions Requirements · Enroll in a Respected Undergraduate College · Cultivate Your Pre-med Adviser · Prepare Well for the MCAT · Apply to Several Medical Schools · Consider Alternatives to Medical School · Dentistry

Part II: Other Graduate School Options · Hunt Those Programs Down · For Those Interested in Journalism/Communications · Engineering and Computer Science Interest Growing · The Comeback of Education as a Career · Consider a Combined-Degree Program · Where to Look for Program Options · Concluding the Exploration · Step Three Checklist

How Good Is Your Bachelor's Degree? · Undergraduate Curriculums for Professional School Candidates: Medicine and Allied Health Programs · Law Schools · Business Administration Programs · Undergraduate Curriculums for Candidates of Other Graduate Schools · Engineering and Science Programs · Nonscience Graduate Programs · It's the Degree, Not the College, That Counts · Ways to Beat the Competition · Step Four Checklist

The Importance of the Tests · The Importance of Test Preparation · How Preparation Pays Off · The Rationale behind the Tests · Ways to Prep for Any Graduate Admission Test · The Nature of the Test Questions · Some Test-Taking Tips · Taking the Actual Test · Consider the Tests as a New Experience · Step Five Checklist

The Significance of Personal Statements · There Are Many Marginal Candidates · Essays for Graduate School Differ from College Admissions Essays · Revise, Revise, Revise · Work on the Lead · Aiming for Clear Expression · A Concluding Personal Statement · Step Six Checklist

The Value of Experience · The Changing Applicant Pools · The Varieties of Life Experience · Writing Up Your Experience Persuasively · Summing Up the Experience Step · Step Seven Checklist

Preface

This book is a sequel to our *Scaling the Ivy Wall: 12 Winning Steps to College Admission* (Little, Brown, 1987). We have gathered much of our material, as before, from the files of the Educational Consulting Center in New York and Westport, Connecticut. Organized by Howard Greene in 1969, the center at first counseled only high school students seeking admission to college or to private secondary schools. Later, some of these students began asking questions about what they could do after getting a bachelor's degree, and the graduate school option became a serious consideration for them. At this point the center began helping people to identify appropriate graduate programs and showing them how to gain admission to fine professional and liberal arts and sciences graduate programs.

Preparing for admission to any graduate program is in many ways so different from preparing for admission to college that many prospective applicants (some in midcareer) are unsure of how to go about qualifying themselves, how to get ready for aptitude tests, how to prepare applications, and how to choose and pay for a graduate program suited to their interests and capabilities. Even recent college graduates should find in these pages the answers to the questions they most frequently ask counselors and graduate admissions officers as they discover just how varied are the admissions requirements and procedures of the many, many good graduate programs they are considering.

We also intend this book to be helpful to the numerous adults considering a midcareer change or transition experience that calls for further education. There are, by estimates of the National Institute of Education, some 40 million adults between the ages of thirty-nine and fifty-nine who are in a transition state in their careers and lives. A great number of adults need further education to advance in their professional fields or to enable them to move out of overcrowded fields or dead-end careers; the fields for which such extra education may be required are as diverse as management psychology, medical ethics, addiction counseling, town government, opinion polling, and news broadcasting.

The number of those seeking graduate degrees is on the rise. We hope that this guide will prove helpful to many of them, and to their families, as well as to counselors.

Acknowledgments

The authors wish to thank the graduate school admission deans and students whom the Educational Consulting Center has counseled for their cooperation in sharing important information so generously. Special appreciation is due Barbara Jan Wilson, Associate Dean at Wesleyan University, for sharing her expertise and insight with us.

The authors also wish to thank Betsy Kramer, Robert Sklans, and David Lever for allowing us to use their student essays and exhibits in this book, and we wish to thank the many other students whose work contributed to the book. For privacy reasons, we have changed their names within the text as well as the names of all other students mentioned in this book.

Introduction

GRADUATE STUDIES — A NEW KIND OF CHALLENGE

Graduate studies of any kind are much more narrowly focused than undergraduate studies with their survey courses and electives in many disciplines. Emphasis on an undergraduate major, even a thesis, does not constitute the kind of commitment that you will be held to in any graduate program, a commitment to your future. The consequences of such a commitment are enormous because they usually determine the direction of your career in a way no bachelor's program does. For many, whatever their ages or backgrounds, it is scary to consider making such a commitment. Questions often asked are:

- How do I decide if I should pursue graduate studies?
- If I should, when should I do it? Right after college, after working a few years, in midcareer, or even late in life?
- Finally, if I make the decision to apply for admission to a graduate program, where should I apply, for what programs am I a reasonable competitor for admission, and what institutions will best serve my interests and capabilities?

These questions must be answered whether you plan a professional career such as law, health science, medicine, engineering/science, education, or architecture, or plan to go into business, the arts, government, university research, or the ministry.

Degrees in medicine, law, and business management are especially popular now. We cite the following cases:

Marcia, a Yale senior, is applying to twenty medical schools (the average applicant applies to twelve), and wonders what if — what if they all turn her down? Will being a woman reduce her chances? She knows that one out of two medical school applicants are admitted to no medical school, and this frightens her, probably without reason in her case.

Armand, B.A., Michigan, 1982, earning $35,000 a year as a merger specialist in a Philadelphia bank, is being urged by his management to apply to Wharton School of Business's MBA program. Will the sacrifice of time and energy pay off in career advancement?

Findlay, Babson, 1979, Columbia (MBA), 1981, confers with the NYU Law School admissions office about an evening program. Having two degrees would open a much broader career path to him than that available simply through his current position as a financial officer in a software firm. His wife worries about his overworking — so he hesitates.

Law, business, and medicine are today's big three of graduate education, but throughout the entire spectrum of graduate programs you will find potential applicants with many of the same concerns. For example:

Henrietta, an honors graduate of UCLA in 1988, has been rejected by Northwestern School of Journalism and advised to get work experience and to reapply in three or four years. But UCLA is prepared to accept her in a master's program in communications. What should she do?

These kinds of questions are being asked today by thousands of well-educated, highly capable people, who contemplate postgraduate training as a means to advance their careers.

A word here about the term "professional degree." While it theoretically refers only to degrees providing entry into such professions as law, medicine, dentistry, public health, veterinary medicine, engineering/science, and architecture, many who hold degrees qualifying them for careers in journalism, college teaching, musicology, the ministry, economics, psychology, government, or the many new management specialties such as hospital management now reasonably consider themselves professionals in their field. The distinction between the professional and nonprofessional degree is technical and need not concern us. We will show all applicants for any graduate degree the best way of qualifying for and applying to the good graduate schools.

You should understand that applying for admission to a graduate school is going to be considerably different from your experience in applying for admission to college. Unlike when you were a high school senior, you are no longer part of a vast national group of teenagers all taking the SAT under the guidance of college counselors. Then, practically everyone you knew went to college. There was no question of not applying for a bachelor's program, no question whatsoever for the good students. You knew that college was an essential step in your career progress.

But you don't have to go to graduate school immediately after college — or ever, for that matter. There is no automatic progression to follow. Your classmates upon graduation go off in a variety of directions — some have already applied to medical school, others have been recruited for entry-level jobs, a few may be able to spend a year traveling or mountain climbing.

Sooner or later, though, a majority of those who have not yet contemplated the graduate school option will consider further higher education. For times are changing. It used to be said that you didn't need a college degree —

before World War II, most could not afford in any case to go to college. Today there are about as many graduate students as there were undergraduates in the 1930s — a million.

"I don't say you ought to go to graduate school, but you ought to think about it," says Barbara Jan Wilson, director of Wesleyan University's Career Center. "Within seven years about 75 percent of our graduates have entered a second degree program somewhere."

This, of course, is not true of graduates of all the colleges in the country. Wesleyan is one of the most difficult colleges to get into; its graduates are achievers, with high ambition and high promise. But we are seeing the rising tide of graduate students and new graduate programs starting to raise all boats in the harbors of higher education. It would be hard today to find a university of any size or caliber that is not striving to attract more applicants to one or more of its graduate programs. The national growth rate of graduate enrollment in general is about 3 percent a year. Yet in certain fields the demand for graduate degree holders threatens to exceed the university supply; a coming shortage of Ph.D.s in the sciences, and even of master's degree holders in education, is frequently predicted by educators.

A LOOK AT GRADUATE EDUCATION

About 300,000 master's degrees and 30,000 doctorates are awarded annually in the United States. There are 1,000 different types of master's, and 60 types of doctorates. Master's are given in such specialties as landscape architecture, taxation, heritage preservation, geotechnology, plant protection, pest management, and textile technology. Some degrees have an alphabet soup character — MALT, M.A. in language teaching; MIPA, M.A. of international public administration.

Three-fourths of master's awarded are professional degrees in law, medicine, management, engineering/science, architecture, and the arts, and less than a third are traditional academic M.S./M.A. degrees. By contrast, two-thirds of doctorates are given in traditional academic fields, while education, business, health sciences, and agriculture make up the other third of doctorates. Traditional academic degrees are predominantly in liberal arts subjects like literature, languages, and the social sciences, but biology, chemistry, and physics also fall under this rubric.

In general, an advanced degree provides a professional advantage in fields as diverse as radio/TV, public administration, geology, journalism, demography. Of course the licensed professions in health sciences and law require a graduate degree (though in rare cases law degrees are granted to those without undergraduate degrees). Educators also point to the "standby effect" of graduate degrees; that is, they may become

continued

continued from page 3

particularly useful when a fundamental change in career direction is necessary due to unforeseen circumstances, such as a plant closing.

Selectivity of admissions has these results: at the very competitive graduate schools, less than 10 percent of applicants are accepted; at the competitive schools 10 to 20 percent are accepted; at a third category, called very selective, 20 to 50 percent are accepted; so-called selective graduate schools admit 50 to 75 percent of applicants. Finally, there are those schools which admit almost everyone who applies.

It is safe to say that anyone, even without a bachelor's degree, can get into some graduate program somewhere, although the degree earned may carry little recognition and the courses offered may be at an undergraduate level. Something like 70,000 MBAs are being conferred yearly by more than 800 institutions, but of these institutions only 200 are certified by the American Assembly of Collegiate Schools of Business. "Many of these programs are simply a waste of time," says a Babson College MBA program brochure.

As more and more college graduates take up the graduate school option, more and more graduate school programs open up for the new market. Some are easy to get into and promise more than they can deliver in terms of genuine higher education. You can waste time and money if you fail to get some sound opinions from educators and people in the field about (a) the academic quality of a program, and (b) the respect in which the program is held. Even big-name institutions have some weak graduate programs. Again, a graduate education requires a big commitment. In choosing to apply to one or more programs, you owe it to yourself to be skeptical about grandiose claims as to what they can do for you.

SOURCES OF CONFUSION

Potential graduate students are among the more intelligent members of the population, but emotions can get in the way of rational decision-making when it comes time to contemplate graduate study. Anxiety and bewilderment are widespread. "It was not easy getting into a good college like Oberlin," says Marvin, a stockbroker in Chicago, "but at least there was a system. I mean, you were tracked in high school, counseled more or less, your parents were on your case daily, colleges came round to see if you would apply, colleges invited you to spend the night on the campus. You all took the SAT together and the Achievements. When I look back on it, I wonder what all the worrying was about. I was just destined for a good college. But graduate school? Where are the viewbooks in my mailbox? Where are those friendly admissions people handing out applications?"

The answer, Marvin now knows, is that many graduate schools do not engage in mass solicitations, or set up at college fairs. If you want a good graduate school's viewbook, you must try to find it in a library or in a college career center, if one is accessible. Otherwise you write for it. Members of graduate admissions committees are friendly enough, but most of them are also faculty members and thus do not have time to drive around making themselves available to you in your hometown. Call them up. Go see them if they are not too far away. But forget about any elaborate admissions system that actively puts you in the graduate school picture. If you want to go to graduate school, you have to do your own research into programs and admissions procedures.

"I tell students and alumni alike," says Barbara Jan Wilson, " 'You learned to research papers here at Wesleyan, now spend some time researching graduate schools. There's the library. And don't be afraid to use the telephone. Start asking questions.' "

What kind of questions? Here are some of the questions often heard at the Educational Consulting Center:

- Is graduate education worth the cost?
- How can I hope to compete on graduate entrance exams in my middle years against bright students who just finished college?
- Why should I study law when there are too many lawyers as it is?
- How do you get a fellowship?
- What kind of living arrangements are provided for graduate students?
- Are sports facilities available to graduate students?
- Isn't it just about impossible to get a degree in veterinary medicine?
- What are the advantages of waiting a few years after college before going to graduate school?
- What value do businesses put on the MBA?
- Why should I think about getting a Ph.D. if I am not going to teach?
- How can I get a graduate degree when I have never studied a foreign language?
- What's the advantage of a graduate degree?
- Does it matter what institution I choose for my graduate study?
- Is the Peace Corps of value in preparing for graduate work?
- Is paralegal work a stepping-stone to law school?
- What is the future of the teaching profession?
- How can graduate work advance a career in politics?
- I hear of combined programs like engineering and medicine. Are there others?
- What's the hottest field of study if I want to make money?
- What impact will graduate work have on my marriage? Any studies on this?
- I hear a law degree is a good thing to have even if you don't intend to practice law. True or false?

- Isn't the cost of insurance making it impossible for a doctor to have a private practice?
- I already have a dental degree. What will two more years of graduate work do for me?
- What did the Crash of October 1987 do to the value of an MBA?
- They say newspapermen make fun of those who go to journalism school. True or false?
- What sort of programs are there in public health?
- I want to be a city manager. Where should I do graduate work to prepare me for such a career?
- Isn't it more difficult for a member of a minority to get into a graduate school than into an undergraduate college?
- How many women get advanced degrees that require math skills?
- I graduated from college last year and now I know I want to become a doctor. How can I undertake the pre-med courses required for admission to med school?

THE MANY PATHS TO GRADUATE SCHOOL

We know from experience that if you follow our Ten Essential Steps, you will probably find the answers to these and other questions about graduate education, but we obviously cannot answer all of everyone's questions, so you must be prepared to do research, as Ms. Wilson suggests. What we believe our Ten Step Plan can do in general is introduce a degree of order and rationality into the confusion you will most likely experience as you try to make sound judgments about applying to graduate school and undertaking a program of intensive study.

Such decisions are often reached only after hesitation, much soul-searching, consultation, and, occasionally, false starts. Because the process bears little resemblance to college admissions, you are faced with a whole new set of considerations.

The circumstances of each case vary. After a year at Yale Medical School, a son of a doctor drops out and decides that he would like to work on Wall Street. What should he do? He was advised to apply to a strong MBA program and is now at Columbia Business School. A graduate of Northwestern Law School does not take the bar exam, and wonders what the best road is to a teaching career. The center suggested he apply to several graduate programs in education. He went to the University of Michigan, and is now teaching high school in Kentucky.

These and others were uncertain about the value of further education, and unsure of what graduate program might suit their talents and experience. We have advised college seniors, middle managers looking for paths to career advancement or another career, women who have raised families and now write for their local newspaper or have gone into business, math teachers looking for a way to get into high technology. A few clients already had a master's degree and were thinking about going on for a doctorate.

By following the Ten Essential Steps, such people overcame doubts and very quickly found for themselves new possibilities in further education — and you can do the same.

Harold R. Doughty, editor of the *Guide to American Graduate Schools* (5th ed., [New York: Penguin, 1986]), which describes over 900 accredited graduate institutions, writes in the introduction:

"Many students believe graduate study to be essentially an extension of undergraduate work, 'only harder.' On the contrary, the basic character and objectives of graduate and undergraduate study differ in many important particulars. The doctorate, and to a certain extent the master's degree, signifies the attainment of a high level of expertise in a given academic or professional field, as well as the mastery of the investigative techniques of the scholar. Achievement of these goals relies upon the cultivation of habits of rigorous self-discipline and diligent thoroughness of mind."

ONLY THREE BASIC REASONS FOR GOING TO GRADUATE SCHOOL

The first question that is put to all who come to the center is "Why are you contemplating graduate work?" Reactions to this question vary. Some say they are doing this to advance their careers, others to make more money, a few covet the added prestige another degree may bring. And there are those who say they just love to study and enrich their minds, but they need advice on how to get back into academe after time spent in the "real world." Almost never do people have any doubts about their aptitude or capacity for some kind of graduate work. Most have little understanding about the nature of graduate school, which is usually envisioned as a continuation of college at a more practical level.

Dr. Dov Ronen, an associate at the Harvard Center for International Affairs, says: "Many who talk to me about undertaking a graduate program have no idea what this means. They have an expectation that graduate work is going to be simply a continuation of their college education. Believe me, there is very little relation between college and graduate school. Graduate school is so different."

Those who hope eventually to get some kind of a graduate degree need to discover first just why they want to go to graduate school. This then is a question you must answer for yourself. We have found only three basic, legitimate reasons:

WHY ACCOUNTANTS NEED A GRADUATE DEGREE

The American Institute of Certified Public Accountants in a pamphlet, "Why Graduate School for Careers in Professional Accounting?," points out that a bachelor's degree is no longer considered adequate training for becoming a certified public accountant. Among the reasons cited are: the dramatic expansion in the body of accounting knowledge in the last several decades, the increasing complexity of business methods, and such new practices as franchising, leasing, and formation of multinational conglomerates.

"Accounting firms need better educated and more committed graduates who can advance to the higher level ranks rapidly," says the AICPA.

The pass rate among candidates taking the CPA examination is substantially higher for those holding advanced degrees. Those with master's degrees also have more job opportunities, their starting salaries are 10 to 20 percent higher than those with bachelor's degrees only, and promotions in accounting firms are going increasingly to those with master's degrees.

Some states now require graduate education before a candidate can sit for the CPA examination, and the AICPA is urging more states to adopt this requirement, in an attempt to attract a higher quality, more professional student.

Any college graduate who has strong math skills should consider the alternative of a master's program in accounting if he or she is thinking vaguely of an MBA. For further information write to:

Public Relations with Educators Division
American Institute of Certified Public Accountants
1211 Avenue of the Americas
New York, N.Y. 10036-8775

1. A graduate degree is essential for going into certain professions — law, health care (medicine, dentistry, public health, veterinary medicine, mental health), teaching at a college level, engineering, library administration, scientific research, technical administration.
2. A graduate degree can help to advance your career — MBAs on the whole earn more money than non-MBAs; engineers with advanced degrees usually wind up with bigger responsibilities and more income; teachers with master's degrees are better paid than those without them. Note that we say only that another degree *can* help you, not that it will. This depends on what you make of the degree; an advanced degree is not a guarantee of a job or of a certain income level.
3. A graduate degree can give you the personal satisfaction derived from

advanced learning. Some work for years on a Ph.D. because they are on a learning adventure and need the guidance and structure such university-based study offers. Many earn a law degree with no intention of practicing law, but because what they learn will have so many practical applications in business, education, and administration.

To summarize, there are only three realizable goals in any graduate program: to qualify you professionally, to improve your career posture economically or in terms of responsibility likely to be attained, and to provide the satisfaction that higher learning offers.

GUIDANCE MAY BE HARD TO COME BY

The availability of guidance for those considering graduate school has not kept up with the growing need for it. Potential students need help as they go about their preparation for graduate work, help in selecting a suitable and

---

LAFAYETTE COLLEGE — A MODEL OF CAREER PLANNING

If the college you are attending or graduate from does not have the kind of career planning offered by Lafayette College's Office of Career Planning and Placement, you might urge that it inaugurate such a program. Services include résumé writing workshops, video mock interview sessions, summer job placement, and alumni contact sessions. Here are selected facts from a report on postgraduate placement for 1984–85 by this selective private college in Easton, Pennsylvania:

- 256 recruiters conducted 2,372 on-campus interviews.
- 63 percent of the class of 1985 said they were fully employed after graduation, and 6 percent said they were not employed.
- placement in graduate programs was as follows:

Medical/Dental/Allied Health Schools	5%
Law schools	8%
Graduate schools of business	2%
Graduate schools, other fields	9%

Lafayette students went on to no less than thirty-nine different graduate schools for academic degrees. There was equal diversity in enrollment in professional programs.

Services like Lafayette's are more likely to be found in the well-endowed private colleges such as Wesleyan, which has one of the best. Some state colleges and universities are beginning to offer this kind of guidance, but the emphasis continues to be on job placement rather than graduate education.

---

practical graduate program, help in avoiding what is known as the "nondecision decision": to do graduate work because you are not sure what to do with your life now that you have a bachelor's degree.

Guidance for high school students applying to college has been a service more or less available in every school system. Guidance in the majority of colleges for students and alumni has until recently consisted solely of setting up job interviews. Only of late have career placement offices in colleges begun to offer counsel on graduate education programs and admissions.

A sign of changing times is the increased activity of the national organization of college counselors called the College Placement Council, with headquarters in Bethlehem, Pennsylvania. Its name reflects the fact that when the council was founded right after World War II, counselors almost exclusively devoted their time to placing college seniors in entry-level jobs. But again, counselors now include among their tasks advising students who are examining the graduate school option.

CHOOSING THE RIGHT PROGRAM IS CRITICAL

It is our experience that deciding on the right postgraduate program of training is critical. Today there are so many ways to go wrong. These are some of the potentially misleading factors you face:

1. The number of graduate degree options is growing. Merely sorting out the opportunities at hundreds of institutions is a problem. Finding the right direction for your talents and interests may require considerable time and introspection.
2. There is often an economic need for graduate schools to fill empty places simply to keep going. You could be talked into a program for which you are not suited, or which may not be of value to you.
3. Failure to do enough research on opportunities in the fields that interest you can lead to your overlooking an exciting program of much greater interest and eventual value than traditional programs.
4. Some go to a particular graduate school because it is a family tradition, only to find they do not like it.
5. There are those who go to law school expecting it to be a continuation of their liberal arts studies of justice and philosophy and not a set of courses consisting largely of technical training.
6. The prestige syndrome can be inhibiting. It is immature to say: "If I can't get into one of the top ten MBA graduate programs in my field, I won't go at all." Not to go to graduate school because you can't compete at the highest level is irrational.
7. There is a tendency to overlook excellent programs offered by state universities at reasonable costs, and consequently to decide against graduate work entirely because it seems too expensive.
8. Inadequate attention to school profiles leads in cases to a mistaken

fear that the competition in a particular program will be prohibitive.

9. The optional nature of graduate work leads some who could profit by it to consider it needless.
10. Misunderstanding about the financial costs and benefits leads to faulty decisions. For example, passing up an opportunity to go to a prestigious institution in order to save money may be penny-wise. Going into debt in such a case may be the right thing to do.

FINDING YOUR NICHE FROM EXPERIENCE

Consider the case of Elizabeth. After graduating from Boston University with a 4.0 average and a Phi Beta Kappa key, she took a job as an assistant marketing director for a mall in Hartford, Connecticut. Having majored in English, she thought she would like to work eventually in advertising, so she applied to the School of Communication at BU and was admitted to a master's program. She hesitated to enroll, though, not sure this would be a sound move, and came to the Educational Consulting Center for guidance.

"I applied for the master's program in order to move beyond liberal arts to a career," Elizabeth told a counselor at the center, "but I've been thinking about law school. Yet I don't know if I'm equipped to be a lawyer."

Going over her college career with the counselor, she came to see that she was torn between the sense of security she derived from success in the liberal arts and her ambition to push forward on a career path. Her application for admission to a graduate school at BU showed that she was reluctant to give up being at a place where she felt comfortable. She was following the line of least resistance and avoiding taking a risk at something new.

Finally, she talked about her experience as a resident adviser during her junior and senior years at BU. "I was a whiz at settling disputes," Elizabeth said. "I could negotiate a settlement between kids who were at each other's throats by appealing to their sense of fair play."

This experience, which she had only mentioned in passing, proved to be critical in her final decision to apply to law school. The counselor asked her to write an account of this student work. With some polishing it became her personal statement in applying to New York University Law School, a school selected because she wanted to study in New York, where she has relatives. In his report for the center's records after Elizabeth had been admitted to NYU the counselor observed:

"We helped Elizabeth see that many of the decisions she had made as a resident adviser, her acts of arbitration and negotiation, and interpretations of rules and regulations had a bearing on her proposed study of law."

IF YOU CAN BENEFIT, THEN DO GRADUATE WORK!

It is our objective in this book to encourage those who would benefit from graduate training to undertake it, but only after spending considerable time assessing their qualifications and aptitudes realistically, and exploring in depth the programs which they consider valuable for their personal development. Not everyone admitted to a good graduate school benefits from the experience.

Professor Heathcote Wales at the Georgetown Law Center tells us that a number of students who complete their studies there do so with little sense of dedication. They get by because they are smart. "They come here because they believe it will be to their advantage in some way, not necessarily in the practice of law, and they are right," he says. "But for anyone to spend three years and lots of money without any real sense of direction is disappointing to me as a teacher. What can I teach someone who does not take the study of law very seriously?"

Unless you are prepared to learn, willing to change your ideas and your thinking, ready to be stimulated by an excitingly different way of looking at the subject matter of your field, you should not go to graduate school.

GRAD SCHOOL IS SO DIFFERENT FROM COLLEGE

In a sense, a four-year undergraduate college is a continuation of high school, a place where students are nurtured, guided, scolded, coddled, encouraged, and shaped by teachers, administrators, and by their peers. Graduate school is, as one professor at Tufts puts it, the real world, where the work load is often unbelievably heavy, the competition fierce, and the days usually unrelieved by organized extracurricular activity or sports. There is little institutional concern for the personal life of a graduate student. The practical side of living is, except in a few heavily endowed institutions, the graduate student's responsibility. For example, it is often up to the graduate student to find affordable housing, practically impossible in a place like Palo Alto or Princeton.

On the whole a graduate student's existence is Spartan, with time for a movie or bull sessions over a case of beer limited to Saturday night. Graduate school is not "the time of your life." To succeed, you must be highly organized, full of stamina, and more flexible than demanding, as in this world the curriculum is rigid and the emphasis on grades in the most competitive schools is enormous.

Law schools are considered to be the most tense places of all. "If you are not willing to work — and work hard — don't go to law school," says the Law School Admission Council/Law School Admission Service, adding: "You can expect to spend sixty, seventy, eighty hours a week reading cases and law review articles." A recommended reading list of six pages is provided before you even apply to law school.

The length of time it takes to get a graduate degree can vary greatly. And so graduate programs are filled with people in their twenties, thirties, and even forties. Younger graduate students benefit from association with older students, but there is also a tension among them — the younger student will have an edge academically because graduate school follows so closely on his or her years of college work, while the older student is liable to be academically rusty but more able to handle problems realistically owing to years of practical experience. Professor Allan Cohen of the MBA program at Babson College in Wellesley, Massachusetts, says: "The older students come up with solutions to management problems more quickly than those who just got their B.A., but they struggle to absorb the reading. I like a mixture of older and younger students in a class. There's a symbiotic relationship. One stimulates the other in a mysterious way."

What is so different about graduate school? It is in part an extraordinary sense of collegiality, of being at one and the same time at the feet of your teachers and working with them as colleagues. You are being called into a learned society, from which you should emerge with an increased capacity for service — to an organization, to a community, even to friends and family. It is not for nothing that we speak of *higher* education, and graduate school is the pinnacle.

DIRECTORS OF ADMISSION ARE ENCOURAGING APPLICANTS

If you are wondering how tough it is to get into a good graduate program, you can find out only by making an assessment of your credentials as compared with recent profiles of admitted classes. Yes, Duke University Law School is tough to get into and probably always will be. But many of those with bachelor's degrees from Duke go to easier-to-get-into public university law schools in their home states, where they plan to practice law; most lawyers they will deal with working there will be graduates of the state university. Those who stand high in their classes in state universities in any field of graduate work are in a position of potential leadership already.

Competition for medical school is certainly fierce. But to be rejected is not the end of the world. The Association of American Medical Colleges suggests that those with a strong motivation and interest in research and teaching in the biological and life sciences should consider entering any of several doctoral programs in biochemistry, microbiology, anatomy, experimental psychology, et cetera. Many of those rejected are pursuing careers as dentists, pharmacists, optometrists, and podiatrists. A few who have been rejected are accepted after reapplying to medical school.

In the sciences and engineering you generally know early in your college career whether you are destined for further study. In these fields the faculty point the way, urging their students to do graduate work in some institution where they have faculty connections. Admission for the most highly recommended students is often routine.

Advanced study for a master's degree in the liberal arts is possible even for students with a 3.0 average who can pass the Graduate Record Exam with a combined score of 1100 out of a possible 1600. To earn a Ph.D., however, is so demanding that only the promising scholar will be admitted to a respectable program.

Yet for all the deluge of applications, institutions continue to encourage good students to apply to their graduate programs if the applicants believe themselves qualified.

Here is what a few directors of admission have written in response to a survey by the Educational Consulting Center:

TUFTS UNIVERSITY SCHOOL OF DENTAL MEDICINE

Here at Tufts we are interested in graduating a health professional, not a dental technician. We expect our students to look at the patient as a whole, not as an oral cavity.

Since 1972 women applicants have increased markedly in the applicant pool, and as enrolled students. I see that trend continuing in the future. The opportunities available to the graduating dentist have been very good in recent years. My office receives far more requests for associates than we can fill.

— Jay Stinson

GEORGETOWN UNIVERSITY MASTER OF SCIENCE
IN FOREIGN SERVICE

Applicants may apply directly from college. However, we are also looking for applicants with business, government, and banking experience whose employers expect them to return to school for an advanced degree. Foreign language preparation is very important in the application process.

— Gloria J. Mugavero

TULANE UNIVERSITY SCHOOL OF PUBLIC HEALTH
AND TROPICAL MEDICINE

Hopefully we will be able to attract more U.S. students as the emphasis on global problems highlights the need for trained people in this area. Our emphasis has been targeted toward returning ex–Peace Corps volunteers and those who have served in international agencies.

— E. Elaine Boston

COLUMBIA COLLEGE OF PHYSICIANS AND SURGEONS

Applications to our school have been declining for several years as they have been at other schools. This trend appears likely to continue.

— Andrew G. Frantz, M.D.

(Note: 2,476 applied in 1987. There were 148 in the entering class. The number who were accepted and did not enroll is not published.)

UNIVERSITY OF VIRGINIA SCHOOL OF ENGINEERING
AND APPLIED SCIENCE

We project a gradual increase in admissions, 5–10% per year for the next several years.
— Ralph A. Lowry, John Lloyd Newcomb Professor and Associate Dean
(Note: There were 226 enrolled in 1987. Roughly half of those who applied were admitted.)

UNIVERSITY OF IOWA COLLEGE OF LAW

Just about any graduate program within the University can have a joint law program arranged with it. To date, we offer the joint program with 20 other graduate departments.
— Dennis J. Shields

HORACE H. RACKHAM SCHOOL OF GRADUATE STUDIES,
UNIVERSITY OF MICHIGAN

We have 21 dual degree programs leading to the master's or Ph.D. For example, A.M. in Economics and Master of Public Policy; MBA and A.M. in Asian Studies (also in Modern Near Eastern and North African Studies, and Russian and East European Studies); J.D. (Law) and Ph.D. (Economics); Pharm. D. (Pharmacy) and Ph.D. (Pharmacology).
— Tina Smith

WILLIAM E. SIMON GRADUATE SCHOOL OF BUSINESS ADMINISTRATION,
UNIVERSITY OF ROCHESTER

We believe that applications will continue to increase (there were 718 in 1987) and that the quality of applicants will increase as well. We expect to reduce the number of admitted students without significant work experience. We will tend to rely less on tests and undergraduate grades as we search for applicants with high levels of motivation and demonstrated histories of achievement and leadership. In short, we are looking more at the "whole person" and relying less on standardized tests and undergraduate grades per se.
— Thomas B. Hambury

TEN ESSENTIAL STEPS

This book reflects the success of the Educational Consulting Center in helping those qualified to do graduate work discover the programs in which they are most likely to do well and to which they will in all likelihood be admitted. It follows a straightforward, rational progression of steps pioneered at the center in which you:

1. Identify yourself as a potential lawyer, doctor, entrepreneur, teacher, et cetera. Make sure that you are suited by temperament and aptitude for a particular graduate program.
2. Gain an understanding of graduate education and admission procedures, in order to determine your preparedness for admission.
3. Explore graduate program opportunities and the enormous variety of degree offerings to see if you cannot put yourself in a stronger career position by virtue of some particular graduate training.
4. Determine your academic qualifications for graduate school. See if you need added credits for admission to a graduate program.
5. Prepare for crucial graduate tests; consider going to a tutoring school.
6. Strengthen your writing skills in order to be able to submit strong personal statements or essays (part of your application to graduate school).
7. Get "real world" experience in a job or internship to prove to yourself and admissions committees that you have a capacity generally for service in society, and particularly for the field you have chosen.
8. Market your strengths to admissions committees. They appreciate candidates who do not display false modesty.
9. Examine the many ways to finance your graduate education. Be sure you can manage your debts.
10. Prepare your applications carefully, limiting essays to the required length, and keep a file of dates of transcript submissions and of correspondence with faculty who are sending references to admissions committees.

We realize that at first glance these Ten Steps may seem needlessly burdensome. Why not just apply to a certain number of programs and let the chips fall where they may? Of course that is exactly what many people do — with mixed results. Simply to get into a random graduate program today — easily, if you are not careful, a lesser program, since the competition is so intense — makes little sense for those who, if they made an effort, would be capable of enrolling in a highly respected and meaningful program, one that would make all the difference to their future.

To conclude with an example, a brilliant student who could have gone to an Ivy League graduate program chose instead to pursue his doctorate at a state university because his wife had grown up in that state and could reclaim her residence, thus cutting the cost of postgraduate education in half and allowing them to emerge debt free. Returning to Cambridge, he sought to join the Harvard faculty, but all he could get was a part-time teaching job, despite the highest recommendations of the state university faculty. "You should have done your graduate work here at Harvard," he was told. Unfair, chauvinistic, vengeful of Harvard, you may say. Or, you may say, imprudent and penny-wise of the candidate.

What taking the Ten Essential Steps can do is maximize your understanding of graduate educational possibilities and ensure for you a career that is consonant with your capabilities. A big claim, but we know this from experience; the Ten Essential Steps have worked for others. That's why we believe so strongly that they can work for you.

STEP ONE

Identify Yourself

THE FIRST CONSIDERATION

Assuming that you contemplate graduate work, your first consideration should be your field of endeavor. Oh, you know that? You want to be a lawyer, or a businessman, or a foreign service officer. How did you come to such a conclusion? Is it justified by substantial analysis of your experience, record, capacities, aptitudes, tastes, financial capabilities, energies? Perhaps not. If these questions arouse uncertainty, that is not surprising. Even the most brilliant often hesitate, wondering if they have made the right decision, measuring themselves, as the brilliant are prone to do, against geniuses or the stars of their proposed occupation or profession.

In the Introduction we noted that certain graduate students find themselves in the wrong programs, and then correct course. Picking an unsuitable graduate program is not always avoidable, and it certainly is not fatal, but it does constitute a false start, a waste of time, and a waste of money. That is why we ask that you take the first step toward identifying the right graduate program for you by identifying yourself. This will help enormously in avoiding impulsive or irrational decisions, such as simply to follow in the footsteps of a parent, a friend, or someone you admire, without recognizing how different you may be from that person and how uncongenial you may find such a graduate experience.

To help identify yourself, we suggest you study and, after reading this chapter, complete the Graduate School Questionnaire used by counselors of the Educational Consulting Center which appears on pages 19 and 20.

What does it mean to identify yourself? It does not mean finding yourself. This is not a psychological test or a proposal for some sort of self-therapy. It is assumed as one aspect of qualification to do graduate work that you are not seriously lost or troubled, for graduate work calls for tremendous effort and concentration. Rather, identifying yourself means becoming more thoroughly acquainted with aspects of your personality that may have a bearing on your graduate endeavors. These include your capacity and enthusiasm for academic work, special talents or limitations, tastes, values, life-style preferences — in short, an inventory of those elements of your personality that are relevant to your expectations for a graduate program.

GRADUATE SCHOOL QUESTIONNAIRE

Candidate's full name _____

College(s) attended (with dates)

_____

_____

Degree(s) received (with dates)

_____

_____

College major _____ Minor (if any)

Faculty adviser _____ Telephone

Grade point average: Overall _____
                      In major _____

Academic awards or scholarships

_____

_____

Graduate Test Exam results _____

Work or internship experience (summers or since graduation)

_____

_____

_____

1. Why are you considering graduate school at this time and what are your eventual goals?

2. What are the key characteristics you hope to find in a graduate school?

3. Are there any schools or programs you have an interest in at this time?

4. How important to you are location and size in selecting an institution?

continued

continued from page 19

5. Will you need financial aid?

6. Do you wish to work and study part-time?

7. Please list your most important extracurricular pursuits. Specify years of involvement and positions of leadership or responsibility.

School activities

	Years			
	Fresh.	Soph.	Jr.	Sr.
School activities:				
School sports:				
Outside activities:				
Hobbies and pastimes:				

Please indicate the one or two which most interest you:

8. How would you assess yourself as a student? What do you consider to be your areas of academic strength and weakness? Do you think your transcript (and counselor/teacher reports, if any) is a fair evaluation of your academic abilities?

9. Tell us anything about yourself that would help us understand you better — your personality, values, background, interests, aspirations, the influence of other people in your life, etc. Please give as thoughtful a response as possible. Feel free to continue on additional pages.

Examples are provided in this chapter of how others have responded to the questionnaire. We suggest that you spend as much time as necessary thinking about the questions and about alternative responses. The more recent college graduate will probably move through this rapidly, being used to answering questionnaires, and so to him or her we say: Slow down. This is not a quiz. There's no time limit. You should provide a portrait rather than a snapshot of yourself. The more seriously you take each question, the better your start en route to your coveted graduate degree.

Going through the questionnaire, the first thing an older graduate school applicant will notice is a request for information about college that may have to be sent for, such as your grade point average, or your faculty adviser's phone number, which you should have available for any admissions officer or graduate school faculty member seeking an impression of you.

Some readers may not have taken any graduate tests yet. Tests and how to take them are discussed in Step Five. There are a few graduate programs that do not require any tests, and even some that do not ask what your GPA was, but these are rare. Graduate degrees are also awarded on occasion to people who never went to college, but this is very rare, and in general we expect that our readers are college graduates, or students who will be college graduates.

Work or internship experience is important enough to deserve a chapter on its own, Step Eight. You should fill in this line honestly; if you have not had much work or internship experience, make note of it. Later on in this book we will discuss whether you would be advised to postpone application to a graduate program until after you have spent a bit more time working or interning. More and more graduate schools, particularly those offering the MBA, prefer applicants to have as much as two or three years of work experience after college before starting their programs. Academicians have come to appreciate the maturity that develops through working or interning.

Note the quality of your work as you fill in this blank. Bagging groceries in a supermarket is not going to impress a graduate admissions office, even though this may be how you have helped to finance your college education. You will very likely be competing with applicants who have had serious responsibilities and accomplishments, like running a camp, part-time teaching, learning a craft and working at it, managing a business, helping a legislator write laws, being in charge of a sales organization, writing computer programs. Older applicants may already be well-paid executives or specialists in relevant fields seeking graduate training.

WHY GRAD SCHOOL?

As we suggested in our introduction and repeat on this questionnaire, the first question you must answer is: Why are you considering graduate school at this time and what are your eventual goals? Here are possible answers to stimulate your thinking, however sure you may be about your response at first:

WHY LAW SCHOOL?

To become a trial lawyer, a corporation attorney, a judge, a legislator, a politician; to become acquainted with the law in preparation for a business career; to become a lawyer working for the government, a libel expert, a member of your family's law firm, a governor, a senator, president of the United States; to become a specialist in taxes, drugs, law enforcement, legal ethics, constitutional law, marine law, military law, or international law; to become a law professor, or a journalist specializing in legal stories.

WHY MEDICAL SCHOOL?

To become a pediatrician, a general practitioner, a gynecologist, a psychiatrist, a surgeon, a member of a group practice, a roentgenologist, an allergist, a cardiologist, a dermatologist, an orthopedist, an internist, an eye specialist; to become a hospital executive, editor of a medical journal, a pathologist, a public health officer, an athletic team physician, a medical writer, a doctor in the military, a doctor in a drug firm, or a medical school dean.

WHY AN MBA?

To become a financier, an entrepreneur, an accountant, a chief executive officer, a stockbroker, a life insurance salesman, a systems analyst, a school superintendent, head of a government agency, an auditor, a banker, a consultant, an engineering firm executive, a college president, a marketer, a plant manager, or a media executive.

WHY AN M.A., AN M.S., OR AN MFA?

To become an English teacher, a librarian, a doctoral candidate in some field, a psychologist, a museum director, a journalist, a newscaster, a writer, a poet, an artist.

BE GOAL-DIRECTED

The above lists of examples could go on for pages. What we are demonstrating is the necessity to pinpoint your graduate school objectives. If you want a Ph.D. in economics, what do you expect this to lead to? Some people are shy about stating their objectives for fear that they will appear overweening, or too ambitious. When Representative Richard A. Gephardt joined a law firm in St. Louis as a young man, he said that he hoped to be elected president of the United States some day, and that he would welcome the support of his colleagues. Years later when he ran, he had that support, and although

WHY ARE YOU CONSIDERING GRADUATE SCHOOL AT THIS TIME AND WHAT ARE YOUR EVENTUAL GOALS?

These are a few answers from the files of the Educational Consulting Center:

An NYU graduate, class of 1984: "After a year working as an assistant in the office of our state representative in Albany, I'm ready to consider my father's offer to let me join his Brooklyn law firm, which specializes in realty contracts, mortgages, liens, that sort of thing. I'm undecided about what law school to apply to, given my mediocre college record. I would someday like to get into politics, though not necessarily in elective office. The prospect of doing real estate law does not thrill me, but the security is important as I am getting married in the fall." He got his LL.B. at the State University of New York in Albany and decided not to join his father, but to become an assistant attorney general in upstate New York.

A woman in Oberlin's class of 1985: "I majored in art history and would like someday to run my own gallery. While working in the business office of a New York museum, I have observed how useful it would be to have a law degree. My supervisor is a lawyer with extensive knowledge of accounting, contracts, insurance, and employee benefits." She changed jobs, now works in an art gallery, and is studying law at night at NYU.

A University of Connecticut man, class of 1987: "I failed to get into medical school so now I am considering a public health graduate program. I am interested in epidemiology and would like to work in a municipal health department in AIDS education, although I would consider a research position if one came up." He is enrolled in the Tulane School of Public Health and Tropical Medicine.

A woman graduate of UCLA, class of 1965: "My three children will have finished college in a few years. I want to resume my academic career and teach. I was a Phi Beta Kappa in college, majoring in English, and have been taking extension credit courses for five years. I believe I could get my doctorate in three years if I found the right program in comparative literature. I am fluent in Spanish, having lived in Argentina ten years. My goal would be to join the faculty of a state college in Pennsylvania, where I live, but I would consider teaching high school." She is in a Ph.D. program at Penn State and a teaching assistant there.

he failed to win the Democratic nomination, who knows what the future holds for a man with such faith in himself?

It is not, of course, always possible to plot your course through graduate school, or life for that matter, with unerring certitude. A medical student starts out in gynecology and switches to psychiatry, a corporation lawyer becomes a merchant banker, a college professor goes to Washington to be a political adviser and never comes back to teach. What is useful about making a projection of your future is that it can help you make the right choice of graduate program.

If you find yourself having difficulty focusing on a single goal at this time, put down options. There are so many opportunities in our system of higher education that making choices sometimes is hard. As you go along considering various programs, though, you will find that some institutions stimulate a stronger response than others, and you will begin to see more clearly what the right direction is for you.

THINKING ABOUT GRAD SCHOOL

Our second question reads: What are the key characteristics you hope to find in a graduate school?

Many people have difficulty imagining graduate school. The term "graduate school" conjures up no automatic college images of ivy walls, letter sweaters, dorm parties, new friends, new ideas, because it is a wholly different experience from college — academically and otherwise. A Brandeis English professor once told a prospective candidate, "Don't think that if you come here you'll spend your time reading beautiful literature. You will be asked to solve problems, and that's a lot different from a course spent just reading Shakespeare's history plays." You may be on the same campus where all the undergraduate action is, but you won't often — or perhaps at all — be part of that, nor will you want to be, because it will appear to be kid's stuff, and because you will be studying harder and learning a great deal from contact with your fellow graduate students.

To know what characteristics you would like in a graduate school, you need to know the range of possibilities. Perhaps the most important characteristic is general academic quality.

ACADEMIC QUALITY

You can assume that the prestigious places like Stanford, Chicago, Columbia, and Yale have the strongest programs academically, and if you are qualified and motivated to study at this level, you ought to indicate such academic quality as a desired characteristic. But remember that enrollments are limited in the prestige programs, so you will also want to apply for admission to some colleges of lesser renown. By what academic criteria should you evaluate other institutions?

One criterion, of course, is accreditation, which at least guarantees that the program does not fall below a level acceptable to qualified members of the profession or particular discipline. Another desirable attribute is a relatively low faculty-to-student ratio — less than 15 to 1. A third consideration is the number of permanent faculty; a program with a large number of adjunct (part-time) professors may be of uneven quality, or it may be underfunded (adjunct professors are paid less than full-time faculty and usually are not entitled to benefits like health insurance and a pension plan).

Full-time faculty can be assessed by examining their credentials as listed in the catalogue — what degrees they have and where they earned them. You may have to find out what their reputations are by asking others in their discipline. You should ask, for example, how many faculty at a certain school garner fellowships from foundations and the government for their research.

Usually institutions let you know who their star professors are, but a key question to ask is: Will professor so-and-so be on campus, and will we ever meet?

THE INTERNSHIP OPTION

Some graduate programs mix academic work with internships. These programs appeal to those graduate students who seek hands-on experience in their field. Drexel University in Philadelphia, for example, requires candidates for degrees in education to practice teaching, and so does Harvard. The graduate student can thus experience the day-to-day nature of a teaching career and better determine what specific direction he or she wishes to pursue in this field. Some decide to be administrators, others to be counselors rather than teachers. Babson College's new internship program offers some MBA candidates the opportunity to spend a semester in Europe, Latin America, or Asia, working in a multinational corporation.

PROGRAM CONTENT

In addition to demanding general academic quality of any program, you ought to identify your interests in terms of some more specific academic considerations, particularly the program content. For example, if you are interested in going to law school, do you want to attend one using the case method of study, as most do, or are you of a more academic bent, preferring assigned readings in law from textbooks, which deal with theory and legal history? This same question can be addressed to MBA candidates, who have a similar option: some programs are heavily weighted toward the study of cases that present genuine management problems to be solved, while others ask you to master the principles of specific subjects, like portfolio management, systems analysis, and accounting; some programs combine these two approaches.

FACILITIES

Facilities are an important component of any program — potentially including, as defined herein: library, laboratory, computer center, hospital affiliation, learned journal or law review affiliation, bookstore, and/or audiovisual center. You must think about and list what you will need or desire for your graduate work — and make sure it is available at the schools to which you apply.

ENDOWMENT

The better programs are well endowed or well supported by state and federal funding. You have a right to expect that a graduate program is not a shoestring operation. It is no coincidence that the most prestigious places have the largest endowments, which means that capital is available for all purposes and for undergraduate as well as graduate programs — Harvard's is over $3.5 billion; University of Texas, $2.3 billion; Princeton, over $2 billion; Washington University, $1.1 billion; University of Rochester, $535.8 million; Rice, over $500 million; Case-Western Reserve, $341.2 million; NYU, $400 million; Duke, $200 million. Institutions with modest endowments, like Boston University, which has $75 million and a student body of 16,000, nonetheless are careful to fund their graduate programs adequately; the excellent BU medical, dental, and law schools, for example, have their own fund-raising staffs and attract much support from loyal alumni.

LIVING OR WORKING CONDITIONS

If you plan to live on-campus, you will need to know what the living arrangements are and where you will take your meals, and you should list now what you consider desirable. If you plan to live off-campus, you must decide how long a commute you are willing to make. Married applicants may have another set of requirements that can be met better at some institutions than others. Do you hope to be able to use athletic facilities? What social life interests you? Are you concerned that there be a church of your faith close by? Most institutions have cultural activities, but they vary. If your extracurricular interest is in music, you may want to make availability of musical activities a condition of your graduate experience.

Will you need to earn money while in graduate school? If so, you will need to find out what opportunities for work are available and what the rates of pay are. Bear in mind that graduate programs demand so much of your time that you probably will not be able to carry a very heavy work load.

PLACEMENT AND COUNSELING SERVICES

Programs compete for applicants on the grounds of their record for attracting job interviewers and in placing their graduates in good positions. The availability of professional counseling staffs can make a difference in the success of your studies and in helping you establish a career direction. By providing access to internships and contacts with people in your field, particularly alumni in the area, a graduate school can act as a kind of pre-employment agency.

OTHER CHARACTERISTICS

There are also intangibles that some graduate school applicants hope to find in a good program, such as the inspiration of good teachers or the thrill of discovery. Some seek to study with a particular professor who specializes in a field they want to pursue. Others say they hope to escape the paper chase after grades and just do good graduate work. There are those who secretly,

---

WHAT ARE THE KEY CHARACTERISTICS YOU HOPE TO FIND IN A GRADUATE SCHOOL?

Two answers from the files of the Educational Consulting Center:

"I am looking first for a good MBA program that will guarantee me a job paying at least $40,000 a year. At twenty-five with two years experience in the Peace Corps, I am prepared to enroll anywhere in the country that has a low faculty-student ratio, professors who have lots of business experience themselves, and a solid placement record based on interviews by top banks and consulting firms. I have a strong computer background and expect a good systems analysis course as well as accounting." This man enrolled at the University of Michigan and is now working for the U.S. Treasury Department at $36,000 a year. He expects eventually to join a bank in the Southwest.

"I want a master's in education from a university that has a special education program. I have taught in a private school for dyslexics for six years, but need broader training. The program should have sufficient depth in its courses to qualify me eventually to run a school for the handicapped or a state department in this field. I expect the program to offer internships and to allow me to take one or two courses in psychotherapy in an affiliated medical school." This woman got her degree at the University of Miami and is now a teacher in special education in the Jacksonville public school system.

---

or openly, are looking for a mate, but we caution them that if this is a preoccupation, their graduate work is liable to suffer.

You probably have quite individual hopes for a graduate experience. Examine them and see how realizable they are in the light of what you learn about graduate schools and your qualifications for studying in them.

COMPLETING THE QUESTIONNAIRE

The remaining questions require less comment. Question three asks that schools or programs you have an interest in be identified. As you learn more and read on, these choices should be evaluated for their appropriateness; i.e., Can you get in? Are they right for your objectives and your personal tastes? Detailed answers to these questions will be better derived through discussion with a counselor or a graduate school admissions representative.

Question four is a practical question about the graduate school size and location you prefer. Yale Law School is small, and so are many graduate programs in academic subjects. Those who have spent their undergraduate years in large state universities often like to do graduate work in smaller programs. Others like the stimulation of a big university with its many departments and the associated opportunity to meet many exciting people.

As for the most desirable location, this depends on your personal situation or tastes. A part-time MBA program must be located near the student's job. A doctor who plans to practice in the South might prefer to study at Emory in Atlanta rather than at the University of Rochester. Such a choice would have the advantage of identifying him to his patients as a graduate of a medical school they know and respect. Weather may also be a factor in your choice. It is not frivolous to do graduate work at the University of Vermont in part because you like to ski.

Question five concerns financial aid, to which we devote the ninth step in this book.

Question six is in a way related to question five; it asks if you want to work and study part-time. Graduate work is naturally prolonged by a year or more when done on a part-time basis. Medical schools do not usually accept part-time students, nor do many law schools.

Question seven asks you to chart your extracurricular activities during college for the reason that this chart provides a record (to be used later, on applications) of your talents, energies, and interests. Interest in aspects of this record will vary according to the nature of your proposed graduate work. A medical school will be more impressed by a star athlete than will a divinity school, because doctors must be strong, healthy, and well-coordinated — surgeons are often outstanding athletes. A law school will see in the editor of a college newspaper a candidate for the law review. Looking at your own record can also help you to evaluate your suitability for certain graduate programs: if you were a major sports team manager, you would probably do well in an MBA program; a debating champion would certainly be justified in considering law school.

Many admissions deans look for the "persistence factor" in a candidate's extracurricular record, for stick-to-itiveness. Being on the college paper or in dramatics for four years is in itself impressive evidence that you are not a quitter and will most likely follow through on your commitment to graduate work.

ASSESSING YOUR OWN ACADEMIC RECORD

Self-assessment of your academic record tends either to underestimate or overestimate your capabilities. Just being aware of your own tendency in this regard can be helpful in guarding against boastfulness or false modesty. The record is there. Since it represents four years or more of evaluation of your performance, it tells a story — if you are prepared to listen to it. It is hard to argue against it with a graduate admissions office, but there are a few recognized extenuating circumstances, including illness or distress over a family problem, and there is such a thing as grading bias.

Here is how one person answered this question:

"I am a strong B student, always have been, in high school and in college. I have never failed a course or been late with an assignment. My academic strength is memorizing and my weakness is writing. My transcript certainly reflects my abilities in most respects, but in the case of art history, in which I got a D, I feel the professor was unfair, and I argued with her about it — to no avail. She and I have different views about the significance of art. She insists that art be judged for itself in isolation, unrelated to the environment in which it is created. I view art as social expression. On my final I got all the true/false questions right — my memory was perfect — but on the three essay questions, I bombed. She said I was stubborn, unwilling to learn something that might upset my own prejudices. All I can say is that this experience has turned me off art, but since my objective is to be a retail manager, this is no big deal."

This statement about his experience in an art course would not have been helpful to the admission chances of this applicant. Such strong feelings raise the question: Would this candidate be a problem to someone on the faculty, particularly a woman? It is more than a frank admission of failure, it is an outburst of no interest to anyone but himself. The young man who wrote it was advised of this and urged to say nothing about art history during the application process unless queried in an interview, in which case he was to say honestly that art history was just one of those subjects that didn't agree with him. In fact the subject never came up. He got his MBA with no trouble at the University of Minnesota, and is managing a clothing store in Chicago.

AN HONEST SELF-PORTRAIT

The final question asks you to be autobiographical. We cannot tell you what to write, save to try to do an honest self-portrait in an effort to see yourself. This is what one graduate of the University of Southern California wrote before applying for a master's degree in economics:

"Because my father is an executive with an international oil company, I have lived in Bolivia and the Middle East. I am very aware of the importance of an international perspective in today's business world. The need among the poor countries for management and fiscal expertise is crucial if they are to develop in self-sufficiency. I would like to obtain the expertise in international banking necessary for working as a consultant in either the private or public sector to second and third world countries."

This straightforward, factual statement, later developed for use on an application, quickly told an admissions committee that this is someone with an unusual background that has shaped his desire to go into international banking. He has picked a goal that is realistic, given his personal experience. His sensitivity to the social problems of poor countries is reassuring because it is unsentimental and linked to the training he hopes for in graduate school.

He was accepted into Stanford's master's program in international economics.

PITFALLS IN IDENTIFYING YOURSELF

Knowing thyself is the burden of this first step toward a graduate degree. But, as has often been asked, with what shall we know ourselves? What is the source of light that allows honest self-scrutiny? It is easier to say what stands in the way of light. There are three things that commonly reduce the clarity of self-vision: revealing too much, overvaluing yourself, and hypermodesty.

Revealing too much means dwelling overmuch on the harsher aspects of the life you have lived thus far — problems with your parents, siblings, teachers, lovers, friends, spouses, authorities, even your health problems. To identify yourself, as we said at the beginning of this chapter, is not an exercise in self-psychoanalysis, which would imply an effort to change yourself. In graduate school you are going to have to get along with the self you are right now. Moreover, dwelling on the dark corners of your soul puts you in a handicapped position, because sooner or later you are liable to bring them to the attention of those you are trying to persuade to give you a graduate education. Educators do not welcome students who may be misfits.

Say your father wants you to be an engineer and you want to teach English. How will it help you to be accepted in a Ph.D. program if you talk to faculty or admissions officers about this family conflict, which has nothing to do with how well you are going to grasp the subtleties of Coleridge's *Biographia*

Literaria? Common sense will tell you that your identity as a student is really unrelated to your father's overbearing character. Better to conclude silently, "Too bad, Dad, you'll have to live with a professor in the family who will never earn half of what you make at the ad agency."

Moral: Without being a Pollyanna, reveal to yourself all your positive characteristics. Forget the demons.

Being overly generous with yourself or kidding yourself is another danger. You win a club tennis tournament and hold yourself out to be someone who could have played on the pro circuit.

Watch out for the tendency to try to get something for nothing — in this case an unearned esteem. This problem can appear in particular among the offspring of very successful people or celebrities. Their thought processes go like this: My mother is one of the top officials in the state; I must have her potential; therefore, I am a born politician. But why did this young woman lose the election to a class office in college? In contrast to the person who is fighting his father's desire that he study in a field that does not suit him, this "born politician" is blindly pursuing an objective that may be wrong for her in an effort to gain the same stature that her gifted mother has.

It really is not difficult to adjust to a different and more constructive self-image when you reject an inflated one. If you just once say to yourself, What am I really? What are my virtues?, you will find it unnecessary to fabricate applause. This realization comes to all those who start thinking about a graduate program — at any age. They learn that with graduate work, there is no way to fool the teacher. Accepting yourself is one appropriate means of identifying yourself.

The obverse of being overly generous with yourself is hiding your light under a bushel. Undue modesty won't keep you out of a graduate program, but it may cause you to aim too low, and not realize your potential. The "aw shucks, I'm not bad at math" attitude, when expressed by the person who has always had straight A's, is not the winning statement he or she thinks it is; in fact it is annoying and is often perceived as manipulative. Failure to put your best foot forward reduces the possibility of competing at your own level.

Having honestly identified yourself, knowing what you are capable of and interested in, you are in a good position to explore the wonderful graduate school universe and recognize places where you fit in. You have hopefully avoided the three pitfalls of revealing too much, overvaluing yourself, and hypermodesty. In this process you are likely to discover what really interests you about graduate study. Your honest self-identification can have the effect of revealing a better, truer self than the one you thought you knew, one that will benefit greatly from a good graduate program.

AUTOBIOGRAPHICAL NOTE:
HOWARD GREENE'S PERSONAL EXPERIENCE

Students who come to the Educational Consulting Center often ask Howard Greene how he decided to be a professional education counselor. He was a strong history major at Dartmouth, and, after earning a bachelor's degree, he started studying law at Yale. While his academic progress was satisfactory, at the end of one year he found that he had no passion for legal training.

Assessing his interests, which included sports (he had been a varsity hockey player), he concluded that he might make a career of education. And so he took a job as a teacher in a private school for several years. At the same time he enrolled at the Harvard School of Education, eventually earning a master's in clinical counseling.

This qualified him to work on the admissions staff at Princeton. Seeing how many applicants and high school counselors seemed to be ignorant of admissions criteria and of alternatives to traditional application patterns, he decided to start his own consulting firm to work with schools and college applicants and their parents.

And now he has expanded his practice to include the counseling of potential graduate students.

Step One Checklist

1. Help identify yourself as a potential graduate student by filling out the Educational Consulting Center questionnaire.

2. Do not think of identifying yourself as "finding yourself"; the graduate school application process should not be looked on as therapy.

3. Be sure to think through your goals and how they relate to your experience and capabilities.

4. Describe the characteristics you would like to find in a graduate program; consider academic quality, program content, internships, endowment, facilities, living and working conditions, placement and counseling services, location, costs, financial aid.

5. Assess your academic record as honestly as you can. Beware of overestimating or underestimating yourself.

6. Accent the positive side of your character as you identify yourself, and carry this spirit over into your applications and interviews.

Understand Graduate Education and Admissions

THE CHARACTER OF GRADUATE EDUCATION

We have noted that graduate education is a substantially different experience from college education. Moreover, little in college prepares the average qualified candidate for what he or she is undertaking when accepting an invitation to enroll in any graduate program. It is natural to suppose that graduate courses will be like college courses, only tougher, and this is true, but it is not the whole truth. There is a psychological atmosphere associated with advanced study that will startle you at first, a kind of excitement that is aroused by good faculty.

In college the professors must share their students with the "campus" and all its exciting offerings of athletics, extracurricular activities, fraternities, homecoming, proms. Professors know the influence of the student center on young people finally away from home and community surveillance. But in graduate school, while there may be some intramural sports, publications, and the family concerns of married students, your chief activity should be the graduate program. If you acknowledge this wholeheartedly, your experience as a graduate student will be highly rewarding. Graduate students who have their doubts have a hard time, and may soon choose to drop out or simply finish their work without enthusiasm and therefore not benefit sufficiently from it.

Any slacking off is liable to be noticed; warnings if nothing else can jolt a student into a realization of the effort required to complete a good graduate program. At the Graduate School of Journalism of Columbia University you are expected to put in an eight-hour day, five days a week, as you would on a newspaper. Once a student showed up for class about noon. When asked for an excuse, he replied honestly, "Hangover. I was in Greenwich Village until four this morning." He was told that he could get away with that reply just once at Columbia and probably never on a job in the media. An experienced journalist-turned-professor told him, "There are capable young people lined up waiting to take your job, and every editor knows whom he can get to replace you tomorrow." With that went the myth of the successful boozing journalist.

Here's how one man, now a professor of accounting, explains his progress in graduate school. "I went to Kent State with the object of doing graduate work at Wisconsin. For four years I knew my GPA to the third decimal place, and I then graduated high in my class, in the top 5 percent. Once welcomed by Wisconsin I never thought about grades again. I had arrived. I knew it, the faculty knew it. We were a good fit. I immediately went into a Ph.D. program."

If you will take yourself seriously as a graduate student, you will succeed, and you can take pride in the new knowledge acquired through hard work.

DON'T FIGHT THE SYSTEM

When applying to graduate school, don't fight the system. Play within the rules. Present your case for admission in the best fashion possible, carefully observing what an institution asks of you. And after you have done everything by the book, think of the enhancements to your application that will make you stand out above competitors with similar profiles.

Graduate admission procedures are more sophisticated and complicated than those for undergraduate admissions. Graduate admissions committees, made up mostly of faculty not paid extra for their committee work, expect that applicants will think more about their purposes, goals, and qualifications, and seek more evidence of abilities and readiness for graduate work.

You can beat the system (i.e., avoid rejection) by letting this elaborate process work for you. Remember that graduate admissions committees:

- make decisions which are more merit-based than undergraduate committees;
- scrutinize what you say about your hopes, loves, passions, and style of life and assess how these fit with your choice of graduate work;
- look for strong recommendations from your undergraduate faculty and realize that graduate programs sometimes admit applicants largely on the basis of an enthusiastic faculty opinion about your work;
- pore over your college transcript to determine how rigorous and appropriate your academic courses are as preparation for graduate study;
- read your applications, personal statements, essays very closely, and evaluate your interview performance to establish your talent for and commitment to graduate work.

HOW PRESTIGIOUS GRADUATE PROGRAMS
CAN SHAPE YOUR FUTURE

Prestige is not an inherited characteristic of famous old institutions like Harvard, Columbia, and Yale, or great public ones like Wisconsin and Berkeley. It derives from the success of their graduates. For this reason corporate recruiters tend to do most of their interviews at the top twenty MBA programs, law firms at the top twenty law schools, hospitals seeking residents and interns at the top twenty medical schools. But in addition, in order not to overlook excellent students, they turn to the very best of the regional schools in their area, with which they tend to have long-term relationships and a record of success with those graduates they have recruited.

In the case of engineering and science programs, the more prestigious schools have more money for top faculty and the latest in sophisticated laboratory equipment. Employers and research institutions again naturally limit their recruiting to the leading schools.

The import of this pecking order of graduate programs is quite simply this: If you have the luxury of choosing among programs of more or less prestige, choose to enroll in one of the prestigious for the sake of your career. Don't make excuses such as: I don't want to be so far from home; I couldn't live in the city (or I couldn't live in a small town); I don't want the debt burden. On the other hand, if it makes you truly uncomfortable to face the high pressure of strong peer competitors, you should obey your instincts and avoid the academic stratosphere where the air is thin.

UNDERSTAND THAT NO TWO PROGRAMS ARE ALIKE

There is considerable naïveté among applicants about the nature of particular graduate school programs. Admissions committees often reject applicants who have not studied the catalogues of several institutions to compare them. Such applicants literally do not know why they are applying to each specific program. Yale and Harvard Law are equally prestigious schools but distinctly different in their methods of training. Some MBA programs now offer training in manufacturing management and international business, while others offer hospital management or real estate development. The same distinctions will be found among graduate schools in all fields. It is the job of the applicant to discover these differences and articulate them in his or her presentations to admissions committees. Letting an admissions committee know precisely what appeals to you in a graduate program makes your application more persuasive.

FINDING YOURSELF IN MIDLIFE

A wonderful thing about higher education in the United States is its openness. Graduate programs constitute one of those last frontiers where anyone at any age can stake out a claim and take up a new life. William Rawn already was a success by most standards — honor graduate of Yale, class of 1965, Harvard law degree, good job in a Washington law firm. But the job bored him, and so he simply quit to pursue a childhood passion, art and architecture. Decamping for Aspen, Colorado, he studied art and made prints, while supporting himself as a waiter. Two years later he went back to office work as assistant to the president of the University of Massachusetts, and then as assistant chancellor for physical planning. His prints began to sell in New York galleries and in Europe. But he still had not quite found himself.

All along in the back of his mind was architecture. So in his midthirties he enrolled at MIT's School of Design, won the prize for design in his class in 1979, got an M.S., and joined a New York architectural firm. Four years later he formed William Rawn Associates in Cambridge, Massachusetts, and he is now designing office buildings and private homes. Readers of *House,* by Tracy Kidder, may recognize Rawn as the architect for a private home in Amherst that is the subject of that fascinating and best-selling book.

"Some people who have had Bill's vita come across their desks see in it the progress of a dilettante," writes Kidder. We see in it a portrait of one who seized the day and took full advantage of the opportunities graduate education offers.

Philip Tobey, Harvard class of 1962, immediately after graduation got a master's in history at Boston University, earned two advanced teaching certificates, and taught in private schools until he got laid off. So did he then waste time feeling sorry for himself? Hardly. He enrolled at Northeastern University and earned a certificate in computer programming and systems analysis, and has completed work for a second certificate in computer science.

Tobey is one of thousands of so-called graying students who are doing postgraduate work, many of them part-time. Stanford and the University of Chicago are studying how to expand offerings to people such as Tobey. Harvard Extension, a night program with no entrance requirements, is training mostly college graduates, many of whom are earning master's degrees. One out of five of these students already has a graduate degree and one out of twenty has a doctorate.

If you are interested in graduate work in midcareer, contact your state education department and ask for a list of institutions which will welcome you. You'll be amazed at the number of fresh chances awaiting you.

QUALIFIED MINORITY STUDENTS WANTED

Declining minority enrollment in graduate programs may mean new opportunities for those seeking advanced degrees. The key to admission is to be a qualified student. Universities are sensitive to charges of reverse discrimination and will not admit minorities who cannot do graduate work.

A student with good grades and weak test scores may be seen as a potential graduate student, as schools may go on the assumption that he or she was simply not sufficiently grounded to do well in math and verbal tests. On the other hand, a brilliant minority student will be actively sought after by great university graduate programs.

To encourage minority students, Rutgers University and Seton Hall Law School in northern New Jersey have set up six-week summer schools where a student can discover whether or not law school is a viable option in a state where only 5 percent of 32,000 members of the bar are members of minority groups. About a fourth of 120 in the program have actually finished law school.

MINORITIES SHOULD USE THE LOCATER SERVICE

Over 20,000 minority students turn to the Minority Graduate Student Locater Service. It matches them with institutions seeking minority students. You can begin using it in your junior year of college.

The computer-based search service uses five variables: racial or ethnic background, intended graduate major, eventual degree objective, state of residence, and geographic preference for graduate study.

Those interested are advised to apply early. The search year begins July 1. There is no charge for the service. For an information bulletin write:

Minority Graduate Student Locater Service
CN 6010, Princeton, NJ 08541-6010

NO DISCRIMINATION AGAINST WOMEN ANYMORE

Times are changing. While the number of women professors and administrators in higher education does not begin to reflect the numbers enrolled as undergraduates and graduate students, graduate programs no longer can keep anyone out for reasons of gender.

THERE'S ALWAYS ROOM FOR A GOOD STUDENT

Returning to Cambridge in 1919 from service in the American Expeditionary Force in France in World War I, a young Harvard College graduate dropped around to get advice about a career from one of his history professors, and was told he ought to look into Harvard Law School. At the law school he was given basic information about the calendar and when tuition payments were due.

"How do I apply? What are the requirements?" he asked.

The answer was, "You do not apply, you enroll. As a Harvard College man, you qualify."

He became a very prosperous Boston lawyer, and years later used to tell this story to young men and women asking him how they might go about entering the legal profession. Being a Harvard College or Radcliffe College graduate can still be helpful in getting into Harvard Law School nowadays, he would say, but you might have a better chance of admission to that school as a graduate from a college you have never heard of, if your record there was exceptional.

In a sense graduate school admissions is more open today than it was in the era when where you went to college counted more heavily than your undergraduate record. Harvard graduate schools often reject applicants with Harvard-Radcliffe bachelor's degrees, while they accept top students from colleges of little prestige. We know of a young man who emigrated from Poland in his teens, learned English in high school, and went to the University of St. Thomas, a small Catholic institution in Houston. He is currently at Harvard Law School on a scholarship.

What is true for Harvard is true for other excellent graduate schools. Today no one is allowed simply to enroll. The graduate admissions process is complicated and the best students are obliged to grasp its complexities and follow its procedures rigorously.

WIDE-OPEN ADMISSIONS

If you look at the list of colleges represented by their graduates at Columbia Business School, you will find among the 600 or so in the class of 1987, 29 from Harvard and 11 from Radcliffe, but you will also find that students were admitted from more than 200 other colleges. Cornell Medical School enrollment is likewise drawn from a broad representation of undergraduate colleges; one medical student had done graduate work in anthropology at Brandeis University, another majored in creative writing at the University of Massachusetts, and another majored in economics at Kent State University.

Examples of this variety abound and show that to get into a competitive graduate program, it is not necessary to have a bachelor's degree from a highly competitive college. Conversely, to have such a degree is no guarantee of admission anywhere except to noncompetitive schools.

COPING WITH COMPETITION

It is the large number of applicants for a small number of places that distinguishes admissions to some of the professional graduate schools — 2,600 applicants for 175 places at the University of Chicago Law School, to take an extreme instance. The reason for this disproportion lies in the recognized quality of programs such schools offer. The value of a graduate degree is not necessarily measured by money to be consequently earned; many who enter a profession have objectives other than six-figure salaries — their intended careers may be in government service, research, foundations, or education. But characteristically the men and women who qualify for admission to these schools make no small plans; they are aiming to be among the top performers in whatever they undertake; they are self-selected leaders of tomorrow.

Yale School of Management says: "Yale wishes to enroll future business leaders, future government leaders, and future leaders in nonprofit organizations. . . ." Johns Hopkins School of Hygiene and Public Health describes itself this way: "The school provides the highest quality education in public health and the sciences basic to it for those individuals who have the potential to excel in education, research and public health practice."

Clearly, only those who have confidence in their leadership potential, based on their achievements so far, should apply to such a school.

TAKE TIME TO UNDERSTAND WHAT GRADUATE SCHOOL IS ALL ABOUT

Your success in being admitted to a good graduate school that supports your goals and meets your needs will depend on your willingness to take time to learn a good deal about graduate programs, and about their admission requirements and procedures. Many bright people start a graduate program without having given sufficient thought to (a) the substance of the program's courses, and (b) the value of the program to their career goals. Why is this?

One reason is that bright people have little difficulty in being admitted to good graduate programs. They apply without much thought, other than that it would be a good idea to have a law degree or an MBA or an M.S. It is flattering to be admitted to a prestigious program. It is pleasant at the start to be back in academic harness. But in time the candidate comes to realize that while he or she may be in a very good graduate school, it is a program that is not good for him or her.

Trial and error of this sort is expensive and avoidable, if you will just ask yourself a few questions:

1. Do I really understand the nature of the program to which I am applying? Have I any real idea of the course content I must master? If so, does it interest me? Will I enjoy it? Will I be willing to give the work my all?

2. Again, why am I about to do graduate work? How does this particular program help me to fulfill my goals? Is this added education really necessary?

Finally, there is the admissions problem. You may investigate a program and apply, only to be turned down. But this happens to literally thousands of applicants, who nonetheless are admitted to one or more other programs and go on to get their graduate degrees. You must know that getting into the right program for you calls for scrutiny of a number of programs, and for sending applications to several, among which there should be at least one that will respond favorably. Failing everything, it is always possible to make up your deficiencies by further study.

We wish to assure every competent applicant, every good student, that if you will take the time to learn what graduate education demands of you and which programs will meet your personal goals, you will surely find one that will accept you, and what's more you will then do well in it.

Step Two Checklist

1. Be sure you understand the character of graduate education and how it differs from the undergraduate experience.
2. Don't fight the system. Follow the procedures for admission to the letter.
3. Study programs carefully, compare them, and apply only to those that are compatible with your interests and capabilities.
4. Remember that top graduate programs are open to *all* applicants, no matter what undergraduate college they attend.
5. Women and minority applicants should consider the special opportunities offered to them at different graduate schools. In general, there is little prejudice in graduate schools, but some are more welcoming than others.
6. Think of your career advancement in educational terms and keep your mind open to further academic work after you have earned your first graduate degree.

STEP THREE

Explore the Many Program Options

THE GRADUATE PROGRAM UNIVERSE

Most applicants do not have time to examine every graduate program being offered in their field of interest. But anyone can easily draw up a short list from the College Board's *College Handbook* or from the series on graduate and professional programs published by Peterson in Princeton, New Jersey. Both are available in libraries.

It is tempting, if you are qualified, to limit your initial search to the more prestigious institutions, but a more prudent policy is to extend your research sufficiently to include the programs of good institutions to which you might apply either as insurance in case you are rejected elsewhere, or because the caliber of the program warrants your application. NYU, for example, has a graduate program in artificial intelligence that is considered to be among the best of its kind. It would be shortsighted not to consider this program, if this is your field, just because NYU is generally less noted than, say, MIT.

Broadly speaking there are two kinds of graduate programs, the professional and the nonprofessional or traditional academic programs. The dominant professional programs are law, medicine, business administration, education, and applied psychology, but the professional list also includes public administration, dentistry, nursing, veterinary medicine, public health, engineering/computer science, theology, architecture, the arts, and communications — journalism, media. Graduate programs in all of these fields train the individual for some kind of a professional career.

Nonprofessional graduate programs, or academic programs, are offered in the academic departments in what institutions call their graduate schools. These are the higher level of the schools of arts and sciences in most universities, and in those colleges with graduate programs, like Dartmouth and Simmons. Universities offer master's and/or Ph.D. programs in subjects from anthropology and astronomy to Yiddish and zoology, with teaching and research being the primary career objectives of those enrolled. Colleges usually offer only master's programs.

As noted earlier, there is today considerable overlapping in the uses to which professional and nonprofessional degrees are put. "In recent years the distinctions between traditional academic programs and professional programs have become blurred," notes Elinor R. Workman, associate director of the Placement Office at the University of Chicago Graduate School of Business.

Thus lawyers may be teachers of law, doctors are often medical researchers, economic Ph.D.s have professional careers in business, banking, and government, philosophers work in hospitals as experts on ethics. Occupational lines are often hard to draw.

It is good to keep this in mind as you ponder which kind of graduate program to take up. You need not feel that you will be pigeonholed or locked into a single field. This is all the more true in that you may later do graduate work in a different field, or you may enter one of the multitude of combined degree programs discussed later in this step.

We have divided this step into two parts, each describing various graduate programs in some detail. Part I deals with the Big Three of graduate study: law, health sciences, and management (Master of Business Administration programs cover more than the study of business administration and train students to be managers of organizations of many kinds). Part II deals with other graduate study options.

------------------------------ *Part I* ------------------------------

LAW SCHOOLS

THE TOP 20 LAW SCHOOLS

This is our alphabetical list based on a survey of law school deans. We have avoided individual ranking in an effort to deemphasize the prestige syndrome that afflicts so many applicants, adversely in many cases, because it leads to an unconstructive attitude, i.e., if I can't get into A, B, or C, I won't go.

One way to estimate your chances of admission is to recall your SAT results senior year in high school; they are a good predictor of what your LSAT scores will be. All you need do is multiply your SAT scores by 60 percent and divide by 20. If you scored 1200 for the combined verbal and math on the SAT, on this you get 36; 1400 would be 40 on the LSAT. Comparing these scores with those from the profiles of top schools' entering classes (the average LSAT score, for example, for the entering class of 1987 at the University of California, Berkeley, was 40) can tell you how realistic you are being in applying to the following:

> University of California, Berkeley, School of Law
> University of California, Los Angeles, School of Law
> University of Chicago Law School
> Columbia University School of Law
> Cornell Law School
> Duke University School of Law
> Georgetown University Law Center
> George Washington University National Law Center
> Harvard Law School
> University of Michigan, Ann Arbor, Law School
> New York University School of Law
> University of North Carolina, Chapel Hill, School of Law
> Northwestern University School of Law
> University of Pennsylvania Law School
> Stanford School of Law
> University of Texas, Austin, School of Law
> Vanderbilt University School of Law
> University of Virginia School of Law
> University of Wisconsin, Madison, Law School
> Yale University Law School

OTHER REGIONALLY ACCLAIMED LAW SCHOOLS

Albany Law School
American University, Washington College of Law
Boston College Law School
Boston University School of Law
University of California, San Francisco, Hastings College of Law
College of William and Mary, Marshall-Wythe School of Law
Fordham University School of Law
University of Illinois, Urbana, College of Law
University of Iowa College of Law (Iowa City)
University of Minnesota Law School
Notre Dame Law School
University of Southern California Law Center
Tulane University School of Law
Wake Forest University School of Law
University of Washington School of Law (Seattle)
Washington University School of Law
Washington and Lee University School of Law

THE STARTING POINT: WHY LAW SCHOOL?

It may seem absurd, but many people are drawn to law school by the glamorous and exciting media images of lawyers as superstar fighters for justice, or as thinkers and intellectuals who establish the basis for legal decisions in the courts. And the prospect of earning a big salary right out of law school is another reason stated for studying law. On the other hand, the prospective lawyer may plan to devote a lifetime to legal good works, aiding the poor and helpless.

Not to discourage you, but to introduce a note of realism into your thinking about a career in the law, we suggest you test the reasons we just mentioned against the evidence you gather from exposure to practicing lawyers. Stephen Gillers, in his very useful book, *Looking at Law School* (New American Library, 1984), demolishes most of the above reasons, pointing out how few lawyers become superstars, grow exceedingly rich, or are able to help people in a charitable way. "The chance is small that a new lawyer will be able to get a governmentally or privately funded job that will make it possible to work for the needy or confront large issues of social injustice," Gillers writes.

Legal work is usually done for paying clients, honorably for the most part but not always, and is frequently unexciting; it might even sometimes be called drudgery. It is usually very hard work entailing long hours. For this you will be decently if not exceptionally rewarded and as a lawyer you are likely to be highly respected in your community. It will therefore repay you now to answer, in your own way, dismissing all fantastic images of yourself as hero or millionaire, just why you want a law degree.

It may help in your career decision to know just how difficult law school itself is going to be. Are you prepared to spend as much as eighty hours a week studying, for example? Are your health and stamina up to the grind? This is a most important consideration. Especially if you have not yet worked so hard, can you assure yourself that you now are prepared to make the necessary sacrifices any law school must ask of you?

WHO GETS IN WHERE?

The answer to the double question of who gets in what law school is straightforward. Admission to any law school is based largely on two sets of numbers: your grade point average in college and your Law School Admissions Test score. You must be prepared to put these two numbers up against the profiles

---

PROFILE OF DIVERSITY

Here is an overview of the 1988 entering class at Columbia Law School, prepared by James Mulligan, Dean of Admissions. For the entering class of 1988, there were:

6358 applicants
1001 accepted
 341 entered

The entering class breaks down as follows:

35 percent women
65 percent men
22 percent minority
   (7 percent black, 8 percent Asian, 6 percent Hispanic)
45 percent entered directly from college
10 percent are over the age of thirty
25 percent are over the age of twenty-five
15 percent have already earned another graduate degree
115 undergraduate schools are represented
38 American states, the District of Columbia, and Puerto Rico
   are represented
8 foreign countries are represented*
   (11 students — 3.2 percent)

*Most foreign students at Columbia Law School do not participate in the three-year program, but in the one-year program for an L.M. degree, having already been certified bachelors of law in their home country.

---

of recent entering classes of the schools to which you plan to apply. With these numbers in hand, you can divide law schools into three categories: (1) long shot, (2) even chance, and (3) certain. We avoid labeling the third category as safety or fall-back schools, because this is derogatory. Furthermore, the quality of students at some so-called safety schools is surprisingly high.

What about other admissions factors, such as your extracurricular record, your essay or application statement, recommendations? These are helpful in decisions involving many candidates with similar LSAT scores and GPAs, and we discuss their importance in Steps Six, Seven, and Eight. But there is no getting around the fundamental importance of the numbers, so let's stick to a consideration of them in your exploration of law schools.

SOME DUKE APPLICANTS ALSO APPLIED TO 77 OTHER LAW SCHOOLS

A sample of 63 applicants to Duke University Law School shows that they also applied to 77 other law schools, ranging from Albany University to Whittier College and including Stetson University, Mercer University, and Pepperdine University. It is clear that some good marginal Duke candidates who were rejected enrolled in far less prestigious schools than Duke. Thus the distribution of good but not outstanding applicants among average-quality law programs is having the effect of raising the quality of these programs.

Who got into Duke? Of the 33 in the sample who were accepted, all but nine scored 40 or higher on the LSAT (48 is tops and one applicant had a 48). Their grade point averages were largely 3.5 or higher. One applicant with a 2.9 GPA was accepted, but his or her LSAT score was 43, and another with 3.0 GPA scored 44 on the LSAT.

Of the 30 in the sample rejected by Duke only one had a GPA of 3.9 with an LSAT of 41. The rest had GPAs ranging from 3.3 to 2.5. Of 13 wait-listed, all but one had GPAs of 3.2 to 3.5; only three had an LSAT score of less than 40.

This highlights a tendency of some applicants to overestimate their chances at places like Duke. We suggest you try to apply only to those programs within whose average GPA and LSAT scores yours falls.

GET THAT PROFILE

It is critical that you know just where you stand in relationship to the competition. To apply to Duke with a 33 on the LSAT and a 2.9 GPA makes no sense. This is not a long-shot choice, it is a waste of time and money, and remember that rejections are never pleasant, so the fewer you have the better.

GOLD COAST RECRUITING: THE SCENE ON THE CHARLES

Fall at Harvard Law School is recruiting time for about 700 law firms, corporations, and investment banks, some willing to offer as much as $65,000 a year to a Harvard Law graduate even before he or she passes the bar. At the beginning of the semester students in their second and third years receive a 1,000-page briefing book describing each of the prospective employers. They may sign up for as many interviews as they please — the average is about twenty.

Well-known firms, like Sullivan & Cromwell of New York, throw elegant cocktail parties at the Charles Hotel, behind the Kennedy School of Government. One second-year student told a reporter for the *Boston Globe* that he had been to seven parties by mid-October, filling up on shrimp, pasta, and quality wine.

A recruiter from the Boston firm of Choate, Hall & Stewart says that many of the partners there are Harvard Law graduates, who find that each new crop of Harvard students are highly motivated and highly qualified. His firm must compete for associates with others in Boston, New York, and Washington, where the most prestigious law firms are. And make no mistake about the motivation of most of the students in selecting jobs: it is money. Only 2 percent of the class of 1987 took public-interest or legal services jobs.

Some students recognize how spoiled they are by so much attention. "This is like being a kid in a candy shop," one told the *Globe*. Another boasted: "I'm not only certain to get a job, I am certain to get the job I want."

Maybe. But a Boston lawyer who graduated from Harvard some years ago says that many of today's graduates fail to realize that once they have signed on with a law firm, they must do as they're told. "We just hired a young woman who left a New York firm after two months at a salary we can't match," he said. "They assigned her exclusively to probate work, and she didn't like that. Despite the big money they earn, a lot of these young people are disappointed and have some adjusting to do."

To have five acceptances and one rejection is reassuring. To have several rejections and only one acceptance is discouraging. If you are five feet six, do you go out for varsity basketball in a college where the average player is six four? Be sensible and acknowledge your limitations.

So, before applying to any law school, get that school's profile by writing to the admissions office. We realize that some readers may not yet have graduated from college and that others who have have yet to take the LSAT. We discuss in detail the question of qualifying for law school academically and taking the LSAT in Steps Four and Six. This first step you are taking is simply exploratory. You can make a preliminary judgment of your probable competitive level based on your performance in school and college to date.

You may, after a pitiless consideration of your chances, decide that law school is not for you, at least at your present level of accomplishment. Better then not to apply at all, or at least to postpone the decision until you have acquired the credentials law schools are looking for. Taking yourself out of the competition does not mean you acknowledge your inferiority so much as it means you recognize where you stand today. The wiser course may be to strengthen your GPA before applying by taking courses in some academic program that will impress law school admissions offices. Tutoring may be the answer to improving a weak LSAT score. If that does not pay off, then you can move on to another field, or get into a paralegal program and work for lawyers for a while. Many law firms now encourage some promising paralegals to get a law degree and even help to pay the cost.

OF MINORITIES AND WOMEN

Law schools in general constantly seek to increase the numbers of minorities and women they accept, but this does not mean that if you fall into either category you are a cinch to be accepted somewhere. Yes, law schools will take into consideration any educational disadvantages you may have had, but one reason there are more men and nonminorities in our law schools is that the numbers of qualified female and minority applicants are fewer. Unfortunately, America does not train enough minorities for graduate work, and women still are not applying to graduate school in proportion to their numbers. These are cultural and sociological facts that admissions offices cannot overcome.

All we can say is that if you are a minority or female, you will never be rejected by a law school for that reason. Law schools are particularly sensitive to the need to train more minority lawyers, who are easily placed, even before leaving law school. Women lawyers are in constant demand by law firms and government agencies, and so any woman who does get a law degree can be certain of getting a good job very quickly — whether she attends law school later in life or right after college. In fact, it is more likely that a woman from a law school that is considered merely average in professional standing will be hired than a man from the same institution, a bit of prejudice in reverse.

SUMMING UP

Why law school? You should be able to answer this question without summoning unrealistic fantasies about what it means to be a lawyer.

- Be prepared for long hard hours of work in law school and thereafter.
- You cannot get into a good law school without the numbers — a good LSAT score and a high GPA.
- Be sure to get the profiles of entering classes at the law schools you plan to apply to and apply only to those with class profiles that more or less match your own performance.
- Law schools are eager to enroll minorities and women, but they want qualified minorities and women.

WHAT LAW SCHOOL WON'T TEACH YOU

Strangely enough, when you go to work as a lawyer you will find that you have not learned all the nuts and bolts of law practice. For example, important procedural matters such as where to file court papers and how to draw them up are left for the young lawyer to learn from experience — which means hours wasted finding out what to do. One young lawyer said in exasperation, "I had to find out about the registry of deeds from one of the paralegals in the firm. That's humiliating." And that's life — life after law school. Law professors simply can't be bothered giving courses in minor procedures.

THE MBA

Among those who have prospered significantly during the 1980s are holders of the master of business administration degree. The rush to get an MBA has however led to an unhealthy expansion in the number of programs from 480 to a total of 600 between 1978 and 1986. The majority of these are unaccredited, and many are a waste of time. Unlike an LL.B., which qualifies you to take the state bar exam, and, if you pass it, to practice law, to be a member of a recognized ancient profession, the MBA carries with it no automatic or official professional status.

The great MBA programs of Harvard, Wharton, Chicago, Stanford, and others we list in the top twenty do confer a cachet that leads their graduates to be eagerly sought after by businesses, government organizations, foundations, and nonprofit institutions, particularly in education. What a good, sound MBA program does is train you in the art of management, for management seems to be more art than science, depending as much on judgment, the ability to lead, and a capacity for evaluating the character and performance of others, as it does on a facility for crunching numbers. The famous case histories MBA candidates must read and discuss are themselves often stories of horrendous management mistakes, caused by lack of foresight, the misinterpretation of information, or failure to understand the mood of the marketplace. How could the great Ford Motor Company have produced the Edsel? And as a professor at the Harvard Business School has said, "How do you teach judgment?"

Yet the necessity for better and better management makes the bright holder of an MBA valuable to an organization. This is why organizations recruit graduates of the top programs and why they turn increasingly to manage-

---

THE HEUBLEIN STORY — AN MBA CASE STUDY*

In the early sixties Heublein, a successful maker and marketer of mixed alcoholic drinks sold largely through package stores, hired a new marketing team with no experience in the liquor business; it was made up of people who had been very good marketers of toothpaste. Their proposal, eagerly taken up by Heublein and with enormous success, was to get into vodka. Adopting the easily remembered Slavic name of Smirnoff, Heublein piled up profits by selling a new generation on the idea of learning to drink relatively tasteless and odorless vodka mixed with soft drinks or juices.

When competition cut into the profitability of vodka, Heublein decided to use some of the cash built up from the early success of this liquor. The Hamm Brewing Company was for sale, and beer seemed like a sensible product to add to the Heublein line.

The question MBA candidates were asked was: Can you justify a decision to make this acquisition, and if not, why not? You might think about this, and then turn to page 61 to find out what actually happened at Heublein.

*Case study courtesy of Babson College MBA Program

ment consultants, most of whom are MBAs, for solutions to management problems that seem intractible to the executives who have usually created them.

If you are considering applying for admission to a good MBA program, and we insist that you apply only to an accredited one, you would do well to acquaint yourself with some management problems and think about how you would solve them, because this is how you will spend a considerable amount of time at most business schools. The case method of teaching is not universal, but it is widespread, presumably because it has proved to be successful in developing the habits of sound analysis and judgment. How would you, as a top executive of Heublein, have reacted to the question in the accompanying case history: Should we buy the Hamm Brewing Company?

WHAT GOOD IS AN MBA?

MBA programs are offered by business schools, but a master of business administration degree today is being sought not just by prospective corporate executives, consultants, investment bankers, stockbrokers, and entrepreneurs, but also by dentists, educators, editors, engineers, librarians, city planners, hospital administrators, and labor leaders, among others. Accountants, marketers, personnel managers (now called human resources managers), systems analysts, financial experts, salesmen and saleswomen, purchasers, and production supervisors can all profit from MBA training.

Much publicity is devoted to the high earnings of top MBA holders, and if you are in their league, more power to you. But what we said about a law degree applies as well to the MBA: Don't fantasize about the fortune you may make as a consultant, an investment banker, or a Wall Street junk bond salesperson. The best of the MBAs earn as much as $60,000 a year right after graduation, but some even from good schools start out in the low $20,000s if they have had no previous experience. Salary ranges quoted by institutions are deceptive because they include the relatively high salaries of those who got their MBA in midcareer.

One answer to our question on the value of an MBA may be supplied by your employer. The trend today in the better programs definitely favors the applicant with two, three, even four and five years of work experience. A compelling reason for this is the willingness of some businesses and other organizations, including the armed services, for example, to pay all or part of the cost of an employee's MBA, which can run up to $20,000 a year full-time. If you are in your midtwenties and your employer offers to help you earn an MBA, that may decide you there and then. And if your employer doesn't make the offer, ask for it. You'd be surprised how well received such a request may be.

THE GROWING IMPORTANCE OF CAREER EXPERIENCE IN MBA ADMISSIONS DECISIONS

In our survey of graduate business schools, we found that the average number of years MBA applicants have been out of college is on the rise, from two and a half up to four. "It is becoming increasingly important for students to have some significant career experience," writes Elizabeth Chant, director of Graduate Business Admissions at Georgetown, where applications are increasing at the rate of 20 percent a year. At Northeastern in Boston, the age range in part-time MBA programs is from twenty-three to forty-one.

WHAT DOES IT TAKE TO BECOME A CEO?

In a 1988 *Business Week* article entitled "The Corporate Elites: Chief Executives of the *Business Week* Top 1000 Companies," it was pointed out that "You can come to the job [of a corporate CEO] from any direction: 17 CEOs majored in English literature. . . . In graduate education, the MBA is the most popular degree: 225 CEOs have one; 118 are lawyers (seven boast both degrees). No fewer than 42 earned a Ph.D., and four are MDs." Below is a more detailed sampling of CEOs and their educational backgrounds, taken from this article:

Aetna Life and Casualty Insurance Company
  James Lynn, President and CEO
  A.B. in economics and political science, Western Reserve University
  LL.B., Harvard University Law School

Citicorp
  John Reed, CEO
  B.A. in American literature, Washington and Jefferson College
  B.S. in industrial management, MIT
  M.S. in management, MIT

Lotus Software Company
  Jim Manzi, CEO
  B.A. in classics, Colgate University
  M.A. in economics, Tufts University

Occidental Petroleum
  Armand Hammer, CEO
  B.S., Columbia University
  M.D., Columbia-Presbyterian College of Medicine

Scott Paper Company
  Philip Lippincott, CEO
  B.A. in history, Dartmouth College
  MBA, Michigan State University

FLEX DEGREES FOR RISING EXECUTIVES

For every new development there's new jargon, in this case "flex degree," meaning a degree, undergraduate or graduate, earned part-time while working. The derogatory term "night school" has gone the way of penmanship and compulsory chapel. Originally only available in large urban institutions, flex time MBAs can now be earned almost anywhere there is an MBA program, with the exception of some of the most rigorous and prestigious programs — Harvard, Stanford, et cetera. One enterprising institution, Adelphi University in Garden City, Long Island, offers MBA classes to commuters in cars of the Long Island Railroad — 45-minute classes as you ride to work.

In 1968 Columbia University began offering an opportunity to senior and middle managers to earn an MBA in two years by attending classes all day on Friday and Saturday and spending fifteen to twenty hours a week preparing assignments. Applicants should be (and generally are) thirty to fifty years old and should have already achieved a notable level of management success. Employers sponsor the students by paying them for time off, and in most cases they also pay the students' fees of $8,600 a term for five terms. Candidates must take the GMAT.

This program is typical of many excellent opportunities for executives to sharpen their managerial abilities in universities throughout the country. You should keep such programs in mind if you qualify now or will in the future. They can lead to more rapid advancement, and it does wonders for your self-esteem when you complete such rigorous academic work in midlife.

THE TOP TEN MBA PROGRAMS

University of California, Los Angeles, Graduate School of Management
University of Chicago Graduate School of Business
Columbia University Graduate School of Business
Dartmouth College, Amos Tuck School of Business Administration
Harvard University Graduate School of Business Administration
Massachusetts Institute of Technology, Sloan School of Management
University of Michigan Graduate School of Business Administration
Northwestern University, J. L. Kellogg Graduate School of Management
University of Pennsylvania, Wharton School of Business
Stanford University School of Business

THE NEXT TEN

(This list may be debated in MBA circles)
University of California, Berkeley, Graduate School
  of Business Administration
Carnegie-Mellon University Graduate School
  of Industrial Management
Cornell University Graduate School
  of Business and Public Administration
Duke University, Fuqua School of Business
University of Illinois College of Business Administration
University of Indiana Graduate School of Business
New York University Graduate School of Business Administration
University of North Carolina Graduate School
  of Business Administration
University of Virginia, Colgate Darden Graduate School
  of Business Administration
Yale University School of Organization and Management

EXCELLENT REGIONAL CHOICES

NORTHEAST
Boston University School of Management
University of Rochester, William Simon Graduate School
  of Management
Syracuse University School of Management

MIDWEST
Case Western Reserve University School of Management
Purdue University, Krammert Graduate School of Management
University of Wisconsin School of Business Administration
Washington University Graduate School of Business Administration

SOUTH
Emory University Graduate School of Business Administration
Vanderbilt University, Owen Graduate School of Management

SOUTHWEST
Rice University, Jesse H. Jones Graduate School
  of Business Administration
University of Texas, Dallas, School of Management

WEST
University of Southern California Graduate School
  of Business Administration
University of Washington Graduate School of Business Administration

---

INTERNATIONAL PROGRAMS

Programs at the institutions listed below emphasize the interconnectedness of business-management skills with awareness of international issues. They are especially recommended to those with language skills or political science or government majors.

The American Graduate School of International Management,
   Glendale, Arizona (commonly called the Thunderbird School)
The International Management Institute, Geneva, Switzerland
McGill University, Faculty of Management, Montreal, Quebec

SELECTING PROGRAMS FOR YOUR TALENTS

There are several publications listing and describing MBA programs that you should consult, but before you do so you ought to know what to look for besides location and cost. Pay particular attention to: the method of instruction — case study versus theoretical learning (Harvard versus Chicago); curriculum choices — are there many electives? can you concentrate in the specialty that interests you?

Read the Educational Testing Service (ETS) publication, *Graduate Study in Management*. ETS, located in Princeton, New Jersey, administers the College Board Tests. The publication gives brief profiles of over 400 business schools.

You should also consult: *The Official Guide to MBA: Programs, Admissions, and Careers* (Princeton, NJ: Graduate Management Admissions Council, 1988), and *The MBA Degree* by Gary Eppen, Dennis Metcalfe, and Marjorie Walters (Chicago: Chicago Review Press, 1979).

Catalogues of MBA programs can be found in public or college libraries, and you can always obtain one directly from the institution itself.

Interviews are rarely given, but most business schools welcome visitors. If you do have a chance to visit one or more, contact some students and get their impressions.

ASSURING YOUR MBA ADMISSION

There is a compelling motivation to apply to the top MBA programs: It is to these institutions that the recruiters largely go. This is a fact of which you should be aware. A perfectly respectable program, perhaps staffed with faculty who have graduated from the top universities, may have little luck in getting many leading corporations, banks, financial institutions, consulting firms, accounting firms, or organizations in general that pay the better salaries to visit. Because of this recruiting edge, the MBA programs with the great reputations draw large numbers of applicants for a limited number of places.

Georgetown has 110 places in each entering class. It will get perhaps 650 applications, of which about a third will be accepted. Of these more than half will enroll in another MBA program. Such statistics are familiar to anyone who has applied to a competitive college. Moreover, competition is intensifying. Georgetown describes MBA admissions in 1987 as having been the most competitive ever.

All the more reason your Third Step should be to explore the universe of MBA programs. This will guarantee that you will find a school that you can get into and at the same time profit from. A strategy we highly recommend is to consider where you want to work. It may be in the area where you now are working, or you may want to work elsewhere. What you should do next is spend some time discovering all the MBA programs in that area, the best, the good, the weak. Then, find out where the recruiters recruit. This information may be obtained from the institutions, but a more reliable list can be drawn up if you phone, visit, or write to companies in the area and ask: "From what MBA programs do you draw new staff?" Sometimes the list of recruiting organizations provided by a university or college may include a company that recruited there once some time ago; it may be that the recruiting practice of a company has changed since it visited that institution. Recruiting is a dynamic practice, affected by events like the Crash of October 1987. Brokerage firms laying off people are less likely to be recruiting heavily in 1988–89.

Furthermore, not all employers are swept off their feet by the great MBA programs, whose reputations they may believe to be inflated or whose training they may just find inappropriate for their particular staff needs. Their experience with graduates from the top programs may have been uneven, while experience with a local program without a national reputation may be excellent. It is up to you to put aside preconceived ideas about MBA programs and get a handle on what the employing community actually thinks about them at the present time.

What you will probably discover as a fringe benefit of this research is that you can position yourself for more likely acceptance where you apply, because you will be able to present yourself as a candidate who knows where you're going. An admissions office choosing between a super applicant with only a vague idea about how the university's MBA program can move him or her toward a goal, and a less brilliant applicant who has mapped out a career path is liable to take the latter simply because of the greater likelihood of his or her having a successful career. It is a case of the tortoise overtaking the hare.

Another reason for you not to be driven by the idea that the most highly reputed MBA program is the one for you is the possibility that you will not do as well there as in a less-competitive environment. Better to finish near the top of a good program than near the bottom of the best. "The MBA is a filter," says Peter Brooke, one of the nation's leading capital venture practitioners, who has a Harvard MBA. "It identifies the promising players of the future. If you do well in college and in graduate school, chances are you may become a good venture capitalist after years of experience. The MBA itself guarantees nothing." Note the observation about doing well. Go where you can get a GPA that stands out.

As suggested, a good work record after college will give you a leg up in the competition. And so will courses you take after college. Nina O'Rourke of Babson College's MBA admissions staff says: "Post-college/university academic coursework can be as important as any other aspect of the application." In many instances, four or five solid business courses in which you earn grades of 3.5 to 4.0 can offset a weak undergraduate academic performance.

You will be taking the Graduate Management Aptitude Test (GMAT); it has the same scoring range as the SAT, 200 to 800. The average scores of those admitted to the most competitive schools are over 600. Scores in the 525–575 range are the average for many good programs. Scores lower than these spell trouble for applicants to programs of recognized quality. Usually there is a correlation between good grades and high GMAT scores. Improving GMAT scores through tutoring is possible, but there comes a time when you must accept a score as a measurement of your aptitude. By looking at the profiles of schools to which you may apply, you can see how close you come to the GMAT average. Naturally, some accepted applicants fall below the average, but if your score is below the average, you should realize that you are a marginal candidate for that school and take the precaution of also applying to a less-competitive program.

Finally, talk to admissions officers and find out where you stand. They will tell you frankly what your chances are. Write their advice down and then compare your chances; see if you can't find a spectrum of places — long shot, maybe, certainty of admission — to apply to. How many programs need you identify this way? Find a dozen or so, and then winnow the list down and apply to half a dozen.

WHAT ADMISSIONS OFFICES SAY

The following statements were made in the Educational Consulting Center's survey of MBA program administrators:

EMORY UNIVERSITY GRADUATE SCHOOL OF BUSINESS ADMINISTRATION

1988 was one of the most competitive years ever and we believe Emory will become more competitive. The strong economic base and opportunities that Atlanta offers will play an important part.

DARTMOUTH COLLEGE, AMOS TUCK SCHOOL OF BUSINESS ADMINISTRATION

Liberal arts education (as a background) is favored. Engineering is also good preparation. Better not to major in business. Economics and math courses should be taken, but there is no need to major in either. Students should develop good analytical and communications skills in college and look for jobs that expose them to the areas of business that are of interest to them or that will provide a good background for their future goals.

GEORGE WASHINGTON UNIVERSITY SCHOOL OF GOVERNMENT
AND BUSINESS ADMINISTRATION

Applications are increasing by 10 percent a year. Of 413 in the class of 1987, 198 are women, 93 minority, 49 foreign. The average number of years applicants have been out of college is 4–5. Competition is increasing. Our location in the nation's capital will continue to attract qualified applicants nationally and internationally.

NORTHEASTERN UNIVERSITY SCHOOL OF BUSINESS ADMINISTRATION

We expect applications to increase gradually into the 1990s, with acceptances running 50 percent to 60 percent. There are five programs of study leading to an MBA — Cooperative Education, 2 Year Full-time, Part-time, Executive, and High Technology. Our worldwide reputation is due in part to our combination of practical work experience with classroom study.

UNIVERSITY OF TEXAS, AUSTIN, GRADUATE SCHOOL OF BUSINESS

Typically we get 1,850 applications and wind up enrolling 450.

UNIVERSITY OF CONNECTICUT FULL-TIME MBA PROGRAM

Of 593 applicants, 197 were accepted in 1986. The class is 47 percent women. This was our most competitive year, but we anticipate increasing numbers of applicants, hence continued improvement in the quality of each class.

UNIVERSITY OF CHICAGO GRADUATE SCHOOL OF BUSINESS

Our 2,700 applications in 1986 represents a 22 percent increase over the previous year. The applicant pool is older and has more work experience each year, indicating that students without professional experience will be at a disadvantage in handling the program. We recommend that students apply as early as possible, since we operate on a rolling admissions process. [Note: Rolling admissions means there are no application deadlines — it's first come, first served, and when the class is full, that's it.]

UNIVERSITY OF VIRGINIA, COLGATE DARDEN GRADUATE SCHOOL
OF BUSINESS ADMINISTRATION

Applications were up 48 percent in 1985 and 38 percent in 1986. This means 2,000 applicants. Class size is unchanged at 240. The average applicant now has been out of college four years. Competition has never been stiffer. We are committed to diversity in each new class.

RUTGERS UNIVERSITY GRADUATE SCHOOL OF MANAGEMENT

We admit three times a year. For the fall of 1986 we accepted 515 of 1,212 applicants, of whom 314 enrolled. Sixty percent receive aid. Foreign students represent 13 percent of enrollment, minorities 15 percent and 37 percent are women. We offer joint degree MBA programs with bachelors in arts and sciences, with masters in engineering, and with juris doctor (law).

HARVARD BUSINESS SCHOOL

The GMAT need no longer be taken. These standardized test scores are not helpful to us in selecting from a highly talented pool of applicants those individuals we judge to have the potential to become outstanding general managers. We receive more than 5,000 applications a year for 785 spaces. Each year 75 students are offered deferred admission.

UNIVERSITY OF PENNSYLVANIA, WHARTON SCHOOL OF BUSINESS

We encourage undergraduates to pursue meaningful summer and term-time internships, in addition to full-time work experience, to develop career awareness and "focus" for the MBA training. In addition students should develop their analytical skills by taking courses in economics, statistics, and accounting, if possible, prior to applying. Finally, students should seek a broad undergraduate curriculum, and leadership within a range of extracurricular/community experience. We evaluate candidates in terms of their ability and "breadth and depth" of their undergraduate training, work experiences, and personal interests.

KELLOGG PROFILE

Before applying to any business school a candidate should obtain the latest class profile (which includes other school statistics), such as this one of the J. L. Kellogg Graduate School of Management at Northwestern University.

Enrollment	418
Average GMAT score	620
Middle 50 percent GMAT score	590–660
Average GPA	3.4
Middle 50 percent GPA	3.1–3.6
Full-time work experience	96 percent
Average length of work	4 years
Average work salary	$28,500
Female students	37 percent
Foreign	11 percent
Minority	9 percent
Age range	21–38
Financial aid recipients	75 percent
Interviewed by admissions	67 percent
Interviewed by alumni	33 percent
Firms visiting Kellogg	316
Total firm interviews	14,000
Full-time faculty	112

WHO GETS IN?

Competition for places in the better programs is growing, but we urge you not to be discouraged. For what is happening is that the level of dozens of programs that never appear in media lists of the top twenty is rising. This is because strong students, rejected by the most prestigious schools, are enrolling in second-flight schools and thereby enhancing the quality of the student body (this, of course, has been happening at the undergraduate level for a number of years). Worry not about making Columbia. Can you make Boston University?

The Stanford MBA program would appear to be the hardest to get into; only 9 percent of 11,100 applicants were admitted in 1986. Harvard admitted 18 percent of its 10,750 MBA applicants. Such startling figures may be used in arguments about which MBA program is the best, but we think they are of limited usefulness in guiding the prospective applicant. If you think you are smart enough to apply to the top business schools, you are smart enough to choose to apply not on the basis of dubious prestige factors but because the programs provide what you want.

MIT accepted 29 percent of its 11,200 applicants, but this hardly makes it easier to get into than Stanford. About half of MIT's MBA candidates majored in engineering or science in college, compared to 30 percent at Stanford. Only 13 percent of MIT's MBA students come from West Coast homes, as opposed to 29 percent at Stanford. Someone working in Silicon Valley is more likely to apply to Stanford than to MIT. Someone interested in training for a job in manufacturing is more likely to give MIT the nod over Stanford, because of MIT's long experience in such training. Both universities might accept both the electronics whiz from the West Coast and the inventive engineer from Detroit, but the candidates themselves would accept one or the other because of the suitability of the program to his or her needs. General prestige of MIT and Stanford is equal, but each university has particular excellences that the other lacks.

What rejection statistics do suggest is either that many students overestimate their attractiveness as candidates, or that many candidates are playing their long-shot schools while applying to others that will surely accept them. We know that so long as there is a pecking order of business schools, candidates face a psychological barrier; they tend to despair and berate themselves when rejected by places where the competition is stiffest. But most of those rejected by the top schools are admitted to excellent MBA programs.

HEUBLEIN'S BEER BUST*

It was Heublein's decision to acquire Hamm's. But for all the smart marketing team's efforts, it proved impossible to make money on beer, and in fact losses piled up until Heublein had to sell the brewery.

What were the problems management might have foreseen? Vodka is easy and inexpensive to make; it requires no high technology and no expensive aging process. Beer must be brewed under the supervision of an artful brewmaster with the right touch, the best equipment, and sufficient aging in expensive tanks and warehouses. Hamm's equipment was outdated. To make a success out of beer in a highly competitive environment, a clever marketing strategy like the one used for Smirnoff vodka was insufficient. Investment in new equipment was only the first step toward profitability. Success would have required years of patient development of a business totally unfamiliar to Heublein management. This Heublein did not realize, and they suffered the consequences.

*Case study courtesy of Babson College MBA Program

Anyone consistently rejected by well-regarded institutions should find out what it is in his or her record that makes him or her unsuited at this time for the rigor of graduate business study. The last thing you want to do is to enroll in some MBA program lacking standards and filled with unqualified students. In the universe of MBA programs, unfortunately, there are many dead stars. You must identify and avoid them at all costs.

INNOVATIVE MANAGEMENT PROGRAMS

MASSACHUSETTS INSTITUTE OF TECHNOLOGY

The master of business administration degree is not the only *management* program offered by some institutions. MIT's Sloan School of Management also awards a master of science in management (MSM) to highly qualified students. Two hundred candidates work with a faculty of eighty-five, surely one of the lowest student-faculty ratios in all of education, and may choose among eighty courses. There is the possibility for interaction with MIT's four other graduate schools — Architecture, Planning, Engineering, and Humanities and Social Science. Cross-registration with Harvard and Wellesley is possible, too.

Another exciting new master's program at MIT's Sloan School of Management is sponsored by Digital Equipment Corporation, United Technologies, and other companies; it is devoted to manufacturing, a discipline that had lost favor to finance and marketing until recently. Consultant Stanley S. Miller, author of *Competitive Manufacturing* (Van Nostrand Reinhold, 1988) and a professor at the Harvard Business School for fifteen years, says, "This program will give an engineer an understanding of how manufacturing can be effectively integrated into the entire corporate strategic planning and integration process, and this is where the future lies." MIT invites bright engineers to apply.

NEW SCHOOL FOR SOCIAL RESEARCH

The New School for Social Research in New York City has a Graduate School of Management and Urban Professions offering master's degree programs in seven fields: urban affairs and policy analysis, nonprofit management, health services administration, gerontological services administration, human resources management and development, management auditing, and tourism, travel, and transportation management.

Most who enroll have two years of professional experience, for which they receive the equivalent of 22 credits in a 60-credit master's program. The placement office got jobs by August for 95 percent of those seeking placement in 1985. Graduates of this program will be found not just in the New York area but around the country and abroad with titles such as Public Relations

Director for the Bahama Ministry of Tourism; Manager, Human Resources Program, Bristol Myers Products; Vice President, Public Finance, Merrill Lynch & Company; Special Assistant to U.S. Senator Bill Bradley. Tuition is about $7,000 a year.

BOSTON UNIVERSITY

What's an M.S./MIS? A master of science in management information systems. As organizations expand their computer systems, the need for trained experts in them grows, and the M.S./MIS program, which started in 1983 in the Boston University School of Management, qualifies you for rapid placement after a year of coursework and seven months of internship. There is also the option of taking a second year and earning a dual M.S./MIS–MBA. Graduates of the program work at General Electric, Metropolitan Life, Price Waterhouse, IBM, and Shearson Lehman Hutton, among other national organizations. Tuition is about $5,500 per semester.

MEDICAL SCHOOL

Because of changing conditions in medical practice, such as the growth in malpractice suits and the high cost of liability insurance, the medical profession is undergoing profound changes that have led to a decline in medical school applications over a fifteen-year period. In 1975 there were 2.9 applicants for every admission, and in the 1980s the ratio varied between 2.1 and 2.2. We assume, though, that there are readers of this book who are among the 36,000 or so who annually apply to medical school or who are considering such a step.

ADMISSION IS STILL A CHALLENGE

The decline in the number of applicants naturally improves the chances of admission for some. But mediocre students are consistently rejected, and it would be a mistake to assume that the average student has any chance of being accepted by any medical school. Nevertheless, the fact is that applicants are being accepted today who would have been turned down in the past. The actual percentage of applicants enrolled has risen from 45 percent in recent years to over 50 percent in the late 1980s.

We still advise the potential doctor to strive first in high school and then in college for an academic record of excellence, with more A's than B's, as many honors courses as possible in high school, and as tough a schedule as possible in college, making sure to take the requisite science and math courses.

Applicants to their state medical schools are usually given preference over out-of-state applicants. Consideration is also given to the academic disadvantages minority applicants may have suffered in their education. (Medical schools, though, are careful to avoid a quota system because of the Supreme Court ruling in the famous Bakke case.)

SIX PREPARATORY PROCEDURES

Most applicants to medical school are self-selected. That is, they know what it takes to get in, and they begin applying themselves in high school in order to be able to enroll in a good college or university, where they seek to stand out both academically and nonacademically. And yet half of them are rejected. It is our experience that your chances of acceptance by a medical school can be increased by carefully following the procedures below:

1. Study medical school admissions requirements.
2. Enroll in an undergraduate college respected by the medical profession.
3. Cultivate your pre-med adviser.
4. Prepare well for the MCAT.
5. Apply to at least six medical schools of varying selectivity.
6. Finally, prudently prepare an alternative to medical school before you know whether or not you have been accepted.

Let us look more closely at these procedures.

STUDY MEDICAL SCHOOL ADMISSIONS REQUIREMENTS

Medical School Admissions Requirements (referred to hereafter as the AAMC guide) is the annual publication of the Association of American Medical Colleges and it is indispensable. It can be found in most public, school, or college libraries, but it is worth owning a copy that you can read over and over, underlining key sections. The cost of $7.50 plus $1.50 for book rate postage or $3.00 first class is an investment you will not regret.

The guide's eleven chapters deal with the following subjects: the nature of medical education, pre-medical planning, deciding whether and where to apply to medical school, MCAT and AMCAS tests, the medical school application and selection process, financial information for medical students, information for minority group students, information for applicants not admitted to medical school, information for high school students, and information about U.S. and Canadian medical schools. This last section provides two pages of information for every accredited medical school, describing its characteristics, entrance requirements, and application timetable.

You will note that the AAMC guide assumes that some who read it should not apply to medical school. "There is a universal feeling," the guide says, "that medicine demands superior personal attributes of its students and practitioners. . . . Medical schools also look for evidence of . . . traits such as leadership, social maturity, purpose, motivation, initiative, curiosity, common sense, perseverance, and breadth of interest. . . . Anyone who is considering a career as a physician must be able to relate to people effectively."

An important conclusion should be pondered by candidates who have doubts about becoming physicians: "If, on the basis of the information gained from all of these sources, students conclude that medicine may be an unrealistic goal, they are well advised to consider alternative and equally satisfying careers. Likewise, students who decide to apply to medical school, but feel unsure about their chances of acceptance, should have alternative career options in mind. The position of the unsuccessful applicant is a frustrating one, and realistic early planning may help students to deal with nonacceptance and to direct their energies toward other productive and rewarding careers."

ENROLL IN A RESPECTED UNDERGRADUATE COLLEGE

Those bound for medical school should always aim to attend the most academically demanding college, public or private, they can get into. These are not limited to the Ivies or state universities on the level of Berkeley or Wisconsin. The best criterion is to find out how recent medical school applicants from the college have fared. "There is no such thing as an approved list of pre-medical schools," says the AAMC guide, in making the point that there are literally hundreds of colleges that send their graduates to medical schools. Pre-med programs include science and math, but a pre-med student is not obliged to major in such subjects. (The subject of pre-med undergraduate programs is treated more extensively in Step Four.)

Extracurricular accomplishment is also a factor in medical school selection. This includes not only the traditional athletic and club activities, but those directly related to medicine: summer and part-time research and hospital volunteer work. Good colleges have a pre-med committee that can guide students to these jobs locally or recommend resources in their home communities.

POSTGRAD PRE-MED

You thought about a medical career, but you failed to take the requisite undergraduate courses in math and science. Well, you can always find a postgraduate school that offers such courses for credit and whose credits will be acceptable to a medical school. An even better idea is to enroll in a program that has been created solely for those like you. Going to class with others in the same position you are in has the advantage of positive reinforcement — you will know that you are not alone, and you will have colleagues to work with in labs and with whom to discuss career plans.

Columbia, Bryn Mawr, Goucher, and Bennington are four institutions offering excellent one- or two-year pre-med programs for holders of the B.A. or B.S. degree. What you majored in is of no consequence in being admitted. These programs, though, naturally want good students whom they expect to get into medical schools and who usually do, so weaker students need not apply. All four programs are coeducational.

CULTIVATE YOUR PRE-MED ADVISER

This step is sometimes overlooked by candidates, who suddenly find themselves forbidden to apply to medical school by a pre-med adviser they scarcely know. The pre-med adviser in the strongest undergraduate pre-med programs has an obligation to his or her institution to prevent weak candidates from applying to and being turned down by medical schools. The pre-med adviser is not a hatchet person. His or her role is to serve the qualified pre-med student, the one who takes advantage of the advice offered on what courses to take.

Example: It is easy for a pre-med student to overlook the fact that only one of two or more chemistry or other science courses offered at a particular school are rigorous enough to qualify as a pre-med course. The pre-med adviser will steer you in the right direction — provided he or she is aware of your existence. It's not a question of buttering someone up, but simply of being a known quantity who can be helped. It is still possible for a pre-med adviser who knows you to withhold permission to apply to med school, but it will be because of a weak record, not because you've made ill-advised decisions.

PREPARE WELL FOR THE MCAT

This is the Medical College Admission Test, administered in the spring and fall. A discussion of its nature will be found in Step Five.

APPLY TO SEVERAL MEDICAL SCHOOLS

The applicant should follow the advice of counselors or faculty in selecting schools to which to apply. The MCAT is sent to six colleges as part of the $55 fee. At least one medical school will probably use the American College Medical Application Service (ACMAS), which provides a common application form for about 100 medical schools. The fee is $30 for one application and $15 for each additional application. Interviews are usually given only at the request of the medical school.

How many medical schools should you apply to? The AAMC guide says, "The optimum number of applications cannot be stated precisely. We know of students who have been advised by counselors to apply to as many as 20 schools and were admitted to all of them." This is very expensive and it would seem to be overkill. Successful candidates we have advised have not applied to more than a dozen schools, and many have limited their applications to eight. You should be able to screen out eight to twelve schools that have a range of selectivity, from the well-known stretch school (i.e., where you have only an outside chance based on your record and the profile of the school), to what you consider to be an almost certain admission.

A very important point to remember is to apply to medical schools, private and public, in your own state. There you have your best chance for acceptance.

CONSIDER ALTERNATIVES TO MEDICAL SCHOOL

Many medical school applicants take out insurance by applying at the same time to other health science schools as well as to medical school. In case of rejection by all medical schools, they may have a chance of acceptance at a school of public health, a dental school, or some other postgraduate school in the health field.

Other alternatives to explore are doctoral programs in relevant sciences like biology, biochemistry, anatomy, psychology, or physiology. Satisfying careers to consider include hospital administration, optometry, podiatry, nursing, occupational therapy, pharmacy, and radiation technology.

The option of applying to a foreign medical school should be considered only with the utmost caution. Good schools are very difficult for a foreigner to enter, and mediocre schools cannot offer a satisfactory medical education. The AAMC guide warns: ". . . the opportunities for U.S. citizens to obtain a quality medical education abroad are very restricted, and the possibility of their being exploited by schools catering to the U.S. student market is great."

DENTISTRY

We have observed that if you are not admitted to a medical school, an option is to apply to a dental school. However, it would be a mistake to conclude that many dentists are would-be doctors who never made it, for only about 10 percent of dentists ever contemplated studying medicine. Dentistry is a distinct health-care profession, and while the college science course requirements more or less mirror those for medical school, the future dental school applicant has usually already decided in college on a career as a dentist, not as a doctor.

There are about 126,000 practicing dentists in the United States. From 1970 until the mid-1980s enrollment in dental schools rose 42 percent. Since then enrollments have been falling. In 1985, for 4,800 places available in first-year dental school classes, there were 6,200 applicants. Admission to a good dental program is thus less difficult than it has been in the recent past. However, the American Dental Association points out that for a dentist, "finding a desirable location [to practice] in the geographical area of one's choice may prove increasingly difficult." It is estimated, though, that by the year 2000 there will be a shortage of dentists.

If you are interested in applying to one of the fifty-eight accredited dental schools, you should know that college requirements include one-year courses in English, inorganic chemistry, organic chemistry, physics, and biology. Some dental schools require you to take a course in psychology, business, or in an additional science. No specific major is required, but about 80 percent of the applicants major in a science; others major in a variety of subjects including business, psychology, art, and computer technology.

Average GPA for dental school applicants is 2.86 in science courses, and 3.19 in nonscience courses. Average recent Dental Admission Test scores (the scale is 1 to 9) are 4.41 for academic portions of the test, and 4.55 for the perceptual ability portion. It should hardly be necessary to point out that dentists must have good manual dexterity and a better-than-average ability to visualize irregular surfaces and solids.

Dentistry offers opportunities to women and minorities. Women comprise 27 percent of recent entering dental school classes. Government studies project a tripling of women in the profession by the year 2000, to 25,500. Minority enrollment has gone from 8.8 percent in 1971–72 to 20.8 percent in 1985–86.

A must volume to be consulted if you are thinking of dental school is *Admission Requirements of U.S. and Canadian Dental Schools,* available in libraries. It may also be purchased for $18.50 from:

American Association of Dental Schools
1625 Massachusetts Avenue
Washington, D.C. 20036

A COMBINED M.D. AND M.S. IN PUBLIC HEALTH

Tufts University offers medical students the opportunity to pursue a four-year program that will give them both an M.D. and an M.S. in public health. Additional tuition amounts to $8,000, charged at the rate of $2,000 a year. To fit the combined programs into the schedule, the candidate does not take electives open to the M.D. candidate. Faculty and staff of the Department of Health of the medical school direct and coordinate the program. Core courses include epidemiology and bio-statistics, societal behavior and public health policy, and environmental health. Students must complete an approved public health field program during the summer between their first and second years of medical school.

This combined program is offered in response to the need for doctors trained in public health and in new problems of disease prevention, such as the AIDS epidemic. Other training is related to the environment, health service delivery, and health problems of the developing world.

The MD/MPH program is offered only to Tufts medical students, who may apply to enter it after admission to the School of Medicine. It is a wonderful example of the new opportunities opened up by combined-degree programs.

A LATE STARTER

Elizabeth Rider graduated from Whitman College in Washington State in 1973 and finished Dartmouth Medical School in 1988. In between these two dates she earned a master of social work at Smith College and engaged in social work in Massachusetts. She has been on the Smith College faculty and was a clinical researcher in social psychiatry at Harvard. She is proof of the openness of medical schools to those qualified applicants seeking training for a career change years after college.

CONSIDER THE ADMISSIONS SPECTRUM:
VARIOUS MEDICINE-RELATED OPTIONS

- A recent report on the School of Public Health of the University of Michigan showed that 529 out of 796 applicants were accepted in 1986.
- Your state dental school may be among the top dental schools in the country; the difference in prestige between a state and a private dental school degree is not as marked as in degrees from law and medical schools. State schools, moreover, are much less expensive, and being a resident of the state you have a competitive edge over out-of-state applicants.
- Even the unqualified have a chance to make up credits through postgraduate pre-med programs.

Part II

OTHER GRADUATE SCHOOL OPTIONS

HUNT THOSE PROGRAMS DOWN

Almost every graduate school worth its salt has something out of the ordinary to offer to the right student. And sometimes their special offerings are not even listed in the graduate catalogue. Just consider one of them, the University of Massachusetts School of Education's Museum Education Project. Here is the only program on the leading edge of a growing cultural phenomenon, the intense public interest in major museum shows of the work of masters and in traveling collections such as that of the Vatican or those of the Egyptian government (King Tut, Ramesses II). This public support has stimulated the expansion of many museums and the development of new ones, which in turn has led to openings for curators, art historians, administrators, filmmakers, community education specialists, and fund-raisers.

The U.Mass. program offers an opportunity to earn a master's or a Ph.D. A plan of study is worked out for each candidate according to his or her interests and objectives. Among the courses offered are arts in education, museum studies, arts management, environmental studies, and community psychology.

"Out of this program will come many of those responsible for museum creativity in the future," says Professor Judithe D. Speidel, director of the project, who invites prospective applicants to write to:

Museum Education/Academic Disciplines
The Graduate School
243A Graduate Research Center
University of Massachusetts, Amherst, MA 01003

Interviews are held in February, and the application deadline is March 1.

The doctoral program of the Union Graduate School in Cincinnati is another unusual and unsung postgraduate program. It is especially designed for ambitious people with master's degrees who are held back from undertaking Ph.D. work because of residence requirements. Accredited by the Ohio State Board of Regents, the Union program allows you to work on a self-directed project; you study in your own region anywhere in the United States, under the guidance of faculty specializing in your chosen field. Over a period of two or more years you attend regional seminars and small meetings for a total of thirty-five days. Faculty, all holding Ph.D.s, in a wide variety of disciplines, are associated with universities and are chosen for their sympathy with the concept of self-directed study.

Admission is highly selective. There is no standardized test requirement. "Enrollment in the Union Graduate School requires new commitment, new effort, new direction, and focused discipline," says a descriptive brochure. Fields of study of current candidates include anthropology, history, physical and biological sciences, management, and women's studies, and the possibility exists for studying whatever field you can justify in your application. The dissertation is known as the Project Demonstrating Excellence or P.D.E.

Graduates include college and university presidents, professors, writers, artists, chief executive officers, psychotherapists, social workers, and public officials.

If you are interested, write:

Fontaine Maury Belford, Dean
Union Graduate School
632 Vine Street, Suite 1010
Cincinnati, Ohio 45202-2407
(513) 621-6444

Dr. Belford holds a Ph.D. in comparative literature from the University of North Carolina. As a faculty member of Union Graduate School, she teaches comparative literature, philosophy and religion, comparative mythology, classics, futurism, theory of literature, and comedy.

How about a master's in management in one year instead of the usual two? Look into Thunderbird, American Graduate School of International Management in Glendale, Arizona, where the faculty specialize in training you for work in international organizations. You need a 3.0 GPA in college and respectable GMAT scores, plus some foreign language capability, since a part of the curriculum is devoted to mastery of a modern language other than your own.

Here is what Thunderbird's admissions office wrote in reply to our survey of graduate schools:

"Our rejection rate is less than 10 percent. However, it should be understood that self-selection is the major issue here. Our applicants are likely to be adventuresome, risk-taking individuals whose many-faceted activities like travel or work detracted from a purely academic undergraduate accomplishment, but which make them good potential international managers. We offer joint degree programs in half a dozen foreign countries."

The degree from Thunderbird is not an MBA but an MIM, master of international management. This school is highly regarded by international organizations, but you should know that the average starting salary of graduates is $27,000, a figure lower than most MBAs expect.

FOR THOSE INTERESTED IN JOURNALISM/COMMUNICATIONS

A degree from a recognized graduate school of journalism is a good, though not the only, way to break into print or electronic media. Formerly scorned by editors who had worked their way up, starting as copy boys or copy girls, these schools now are visited by recruiters for newspapers, magazines, radio-TV news departments, government and corporate communications departments, and public relations firms. Various departments of the federal government send government employees to certain schools of journalism, such as Boston University's School of Public Communication, for training as public affairs officers.

In general these one-year or two-year programs offer a master's degree; Ph.D. programs are intended mostly for those who plan a college teaching career in journalism/communications. Basic courses include news and feature writing, copyediting, headline writing, page makeup and graphic design; among the electives are magazine writing, news photography, opinion polling, investigative reporting, and book, film, play, and arts reviewing. Candidates interested in public relations can take courses in writing releases, planning a press conference, and product promotion.

Desirable preparation for journalism school is usually a B.A. degree in history, English, political science, or sociology. But the current demand for science and technology writers provides an opportunity for those who have majored in science or engineering to move into journalism/communications.

A good example of a fine program is found at Indiana University, Bloomington, School of Journalism, ranked highly in this field. "Our emphasis in the professional M.A. program is on public affairs reporting," says David Nord, director of graduate studies. "Our philosophy is to balance professional skills training with solid academic study." Joint-degree programs are offered with the department of library science (MLS) and other departments of this great state university.

Admission to this school is competitive — average GRE scores of those accepted are 610 verbal, 580 quantitative. Note that an undergraduate major in journalism is acceptable, but liberal arts majors are preferred.

Many who enroll in graduate journalism programs additionally already have some experience in journalism/communications. With the increase in the number of women in this field, it has become a more viable midlife career option for those whose children are grown. Some women find that after earning a master's degree in journalism that they can get good jobs on local papers or with local radio or TV stations.

GOURMAN'S RANKING OF JOURNALISM SCHOOLS

The following ranking from *The Gourman Report: Graduate and Professional School Programs,* published annually in Los Angeles, is a widely accepted assessment of journalism schools, but it should not be taken to mean that regional journalism programs, especially those in state universities like the University of Washington, are not turning out highly competent and successful media specialists. Also, those interested in TV news careers should look at places which specialize in this sort of training, like Emerson College in Boston.

A RATING OF GRADUATE PROGRAMS IN JOURNALISM
Leading Institutions

Twenty institutions with scores in the 4.0–5.0 range, in rank order*

Institution	Rank	Score	Curriculum	Faculty Instruction	Faculty Research	Library Resources (Journalism)
Columbia	1	4.94	4.94	4.95	4.93	4.93
Northwestern	2	4.93	4.93	4.94	4.92	4.92
Missouri (Columbia)	3	4.92	4.92	4.93	4.91	4.91
Minnesota (Minneapolis)	4	4.90	4.90	4.92	4.90	4.88
Illinois (Urbana)	5	4.88	4.87	4.91	4.88	4.86
Wisconsin (Madison)	6	4.85	4.85	4.90	4.84	4.83
Michigan (Ann Arbor)	7	4.84	4.82	4.89	4.83	4.81
Stanford	8	4.82	4.80	4.86	4.81	4.79
Indiana (Bloomington)	9	4.80	4.79	4.85	4.80	4.74
Texas (Austin)	10	4.77	4.76	4.83	4.79	4.71

Institution	Rank	Score	Curriculum	Faculty Instruction	Faculty Research	Library Resources (Journalism)
Iowa (Iowa City)	11	4.75	4.72	4.82	4.75	4.70
Maryland (College Park)	12	4.73	4.70	4.80	4.73	4.67
N.Y.U.	13	4.70	4.68	4.77	4.72	4.61
Boston U.	14	4.66	4.63	4.73	4.69	4.60
Ohio State	15	4.63	4.62	4.70	4.65	4.56
Wayne State	16	4.59	4.59	4.64	4.61	4.50
Syracuse	17	4.54	4.55	4.60	4.57	4.45
Michigan State	18	4.51	4.53	4.58	4.52	4.41
North Carolina (Chapel Hill)	19	4.48	4.50	4.54	4.47	4.39
Penn State (University Park)	20	4.44	4.48	4.51	4.43	4.34

*The Gourman ranking system is based on a 1 to 5 scale, 5 being the highest ranking in any category.

ENGINEERING AND COMPUTER SCIENCE INTEREST GROWING

Engineers and computer scientists, of all college graduates, seem best to know where they are going. Yet even they should not lock themselves into preconceived notions of where they should continue to study without investigating other opportunities. For example, anyone interested in artificial intelligence should examine NYU's program or Carnegie-Mellon's. The most prestigious institutions do not necessarily offer the best training in all fields. Nor does an engineering bachelor's degree oblige you to go to engineering school for graduate work. A fourth of the recent graduates of the Thayer School of Engineering at Dartmouth went directly into business, while another fourth went to medical school, law school, or architecture school.

The trend in the number of applications to engineering graduate schools is on the rise and promises to increase by 5 to 10 percent a year through the 1990s. This means stiffer competition. At Cal Tech only 207 of 1,649 applicants to graduate engineering programs were accepted in 1987.

The University of Pennsylvania reports that an increasing number of applicants from other fields, such as biomedical science, are applying to the graduate engineering school. At Penn there are four master's and four Ph.D. joint-degree programs offered. Virginia also offers a joint-degree program: a Ph.D. in biomedical engineering and an M.D.

More women are enrolling in engineering, and we encourage more women to apply, because they will receive favorable treatment, however abhorrent tilting to one sex or to minorities is to some white male applicants. In the

1987 class of 25 at Case Western Reserve's program in computer engineering and science, 14 were women. At MIT, only 22 out of 135 were women, and only 7 were minority students in the class of 1987.

Computer science programs are even harder to get into than traditional engineering programs. At the University of Virginia, of 133 applicants to the graduate computer science program in 1987, only 50 were accepted, and their GRE scores were slightly higher than those of the traditional engineering applicants, more than half of whom were accepted — 1280 versus 1230.

The Computer Science Graduate Program at Rice University accepted only 21 of 216 applicants. All in the class of 1987 were in the top 10 percent of their college classes. As applications increase in coming years, Rice expects to reduce the number of students it will admit as candidates for the master's degree, and more Ph.D. candidates will be enrolled.

Competition at great state engineering schools is also fierce. Of 1,000 applicants to Berkeley, fewer than 10 percent were admitted. Unlike most engineering schools, which rank quality of college curriculum as the most important factor in admissions decisions, MIT, Berkeley, and Cal Tech consider faculty recommendations foremost.

In response to our questionnaire, two faculty members on the Cal Tech admissions committee made this interesting comment:

"In the future there will be less emphasis on test scores and greater emphasis on extracurricular activities. Admissions will become even more competitive as the number of applications grows while the admitted number decreases. Expect to see fewer foreign students admitted. There will be more aggressive recruitment of minorities and, to a lesser extent, women. White males will have to walk on water to be assured of admission."

We call attention to the fact that not a single student has been taken from MIT's waiting list in seven years. But possibly the prize for stiff competition should be awarded Carnegie-Mellon's Department of Computer Science, which accepted only 54 out of 882 applicants in 1987. The high number of applicants reflects in part the promise of a graduate fellowship to all admitted, covering tuition and living allowance. The promise of excellence in original research is the primary criterion for admission here.

THE COMEBACK OF EDUCATION AS A CAREER

In the sixties education was cynically adopted as a career by many men as a means for escaping the draft and service in Vietnam. In the eighties education has recovered its traditional nobility of purpose in the eyes of graduate students, and at the same time it has become more remunerative at all levels. The U.S. Department of Education is engaging in a national campaign to publicize the need for more good teachers to keep the country competitive. For members of minority groups in particular, the opportunities in education are enormous because of the growing recognition that they should have equal opportunities in the teaching profession.

Teaching is not the whole story either. An education degree can lead to work in administration, special education, guidance and counseling, language training, learning disabilities, psychology, consulting in curriculum planning. When you adopt education as a career you can become valuable to businesses, the government, consulting firms, the military, in fact to any organization that has an educational focus. For example, high-tech companies like Digital Equipment Corporation have multimillion-dollar education departments for training users of their hardware and software. The U.S. State Department has its own language schools, where employees are taught fluency in a number of languages. Arthur D. Little, the well-known consulting firm in Cambridge, Massachusetts, is licensed to grant master's degrees in management to executives taking courses offered by staff engineers, scientists, and management consultants.

The following is a partial list of universities offering masters and doctoral programs in education: Harvard, Columbia Teacher's College, University of Pennsylvania, Pennsylvania State University, Stanford, Johns Hopkins, NYU, Vanderbilt, Northwestern, Berkeley, UCLA, Michigan, North Carolina, Texas, Wisconsin, Virginia, and Rochester.

A plus for the average graduate student in education: Once admitted to a major institution, you have access to all of its resources for interdisciplinary study. This allows you to combine a professional degree with pursuit of an academic interest in art, literature, music, or some other subject that you would like to specialize in. Educational training should not be conceived as limited to "dry" techniques of teaching, administering, counseling, et cetera. Educators are often expected to know an academic field well and are encouraged to work out their own combination of courses.

CONSIDER A COMBINED-DEGREE PROGRAM

"Over the past decade there has been a dramatic increase in both the number and variety of graduate-level combined-degree programs created to bridge the gap between different specialized fields." So begins the introduction to *The Combined-Degree Programs Directory,* in the *Peterson's Graduate and Professional Programs: An Overview.* The directory lists programs and institutions where the programs are offered, from aeronautical sciences/aviation management (MAS/MAM) to urban regional planning/social work (MUP/ MSW, M.A./MSW, M.A./MSSW, M.S./M.S., M.P./MSW).

Some combined programs are more common than others. Biomedical sciences/dentistry combined degrees are offered at fifty-eight institutions. Only Yale offers architecture/environmental design. The combination of business administration/law can lead to any one of eight different combined degrees: MBA/J.D., MBA/LL.B., M.S./J.D., M.A./J.D., M.M./J.D., MMGT/J.D.,

MPPM/J.D., Ph.D./J.D. These are offered in universities across the country, from Albany Law School of Union University to Yale University to almost all state universities.

Combined degrees that are half MBA can be earned in accounting, aeronautical sciences, American studies, arts administration, communications, computer science, decision science, dentistry, economics, education, educational administration, English literature, environmental studies, European studies, forestry, French studies, geography, German, history, industrial engineering, international studies, Latin American studies, law, mathematics, operations research, optometry, organizational behavior, pharmacy, philosophy, public health, religion, social services administration, Spanish, theology, and veterinary medicine.

It may surprise you to find that there are twelve combined degrees that involve work in library science (MSLS). Public policy can be combined with a number of disciplines, including, for example, administration/gerontology (MPA/MSG, MPA/M.S.).There is a combined-degree program at Pennsylvania College of Podiatric Medicine in podiatry/bioengineering (DPM/Ph.D.).

The advantage of a combined-degree program is that it gives you a unique background that can make you more valuable in the job marketplace. Naturally, only very strong students are admitted to most of these programs because of the prerequisites needed and because the academic demands of the programs call for considerable self-discipline.

If you are looking for a challenge and think you can meet it, look at the combined-degree programs list on pages 194–205 of *Peterson's Graduate and Professional Programs: An Overview,* available in libraries. This volume may also be purchased for $19.95 at bookstores, or from Peterson's Guide, P.O. Box 2123, Princeton, NJ 08543-2123.

WHERE TO LOOK FOR PROGRAM OPTIONS

We have discussed a few programs at random simply to prime the pump of your imagination. Now it's up to you to do some exploring. Begin in a good library and look at a variety of graduate school catalogues, places you never before considered, just to see what is out there. Talk to people in your field of interest, find out where they did their graduate work and where people now are doing it. Read the education pages of newspapers and magazines, and don't balk at the ads. An ad for a graduate program does not mean the institution is broke and desperate for warm bodies. Good institutions compete for good students. USC wants you to go there and not to UCLA.

Again, talk to people. Some good programs may just be getting started and not yet be listed in standard guides. By keeping your ear to the ground, you may learn of just the right program for you.

Ten years after getting a law degree at NYU Robert Vanni went to Columbia for an MBA, in order to strengthen his managerial know-how. He is now general counsel to the New York Public Library.

A dentist we know is earning her MBA at Northeastern University in order to become a management consultant to dentists who need help in setting up their offices and running them profitably.

Roger B. Smith, Chief Executive Officer of General Motors, is quoted in a University of Pennsylvania brochure as saying our society needs thinkers, analysts, and organizers. "These mental processes can be acquired and sharpened by the study of the liberal arts," he concludes. In response, Penn offers its Master of Arts and Professional Studies Program. This program combines a liberal arts or science major with courses in business, communications, or quantitative planning and analysis. Students do an internship in business, government, or a nonprofit organization, and take part in the Colloquium on Work and Liberal Learning, where they explore the relationship between academic studies and nonacademic professions.

This exciting kind of graduate work reflects the expansive mood of today's universities, as they strive to bring their training into consonance with the needs of individuals and of society as a whole.

CONCLUDING THE EXPLORATION

This long Step Three has led you to explore a number of graduate opportunities open to qualified students. Some are like inlets on a strange coastline that you simply pass by during an expedition. If you have no medical aspirations, you perhaps skipped the pages on medical schools. If you read everything in this step, you probably perceived a common thread that runs through all graduate school admissions: Every graduate school depends on new students every year, and the better schools set demanding admission standards that put American graduate education at the summit on a worldwide basis. Nowhere else will a student find such an enormous variety of graduate program offerings. Nowhere else is it as feasible for the ambitious person to enhance a career or enrich life for himself or herself by earning a graduate degree.

Recently a young woman with a bachelor's degree from Pomona College came to see us. After three years on the marketing staff of a Texas software firm, she found herself, as she put it, "somewhat illiterate about corporate management," but she was not drawn to MBA programs she had looked into. Weren't there other opportunities available to her? she wondered. There were, but she had not done enough exploring.

It was suggested she apply to several master's programs in industrial psychology, programs which seek to attract more women candidates. Graduates of such programs readily find jobs in industry or with consulting firms. Admitted to several, she enrolled at the University of California at Los Angeles.

The very multiplicity of graduate school opportunities is overwhelming to many would-be graduate students. The exploration process may seem like a superhighway lacking exit signs. In reality, the signs are there, but you have to look behind obstacles that hide them. You will find that a diligent search can be thoroughly rewarding.

STEP THREE CHECKLIST

1. Explore beyond the better professional degree programs, being sure not to overlook the excellent regional programs that are less costly and more open to in-state applicants.
2. Always get profiles of most recent entering classes in programs you are considering and compare them with your academic and nonacademic credentials to see where admission opportunities lie for you.
3. Explore beyond conventional degree programs for unique programs that may give you a special advantage — especially combined-degree programs.
4. Look for program options in the *College Handbook, Peterson's Guides to Graduate Study,* in graduate school catalogues, in ads, and talk to people for hints and tips on special programs like the University of Massachusetts Museum Education Project, which is not listed in any catalogue.

STEP FOUR

Determine Your Academic Qualifications

HOW GOOD IS YOUR BACHELOR'S DEGREE?

As we've said, anyone with a bachelor's degree can get into some kind of a graduate program somewhere. Many colleges and universities are actively seeking out potential graduate students because they need the enrollment, either for revenue or to justify their programs. Inevitably, whatever the value and prestige of such programs may have been, they are now diminished, even though the faculty and instruction may be adequate. Less-qualified students drag graduate schools down. Beware, then, of enrolling in programs that seem easy to get into. The program you want should make demands on its applicants. Rather than try to fill their programs with mediocre applicants, the better institutions close down those programs that are not attracting enrollment. Georgetown and Boston University have closed their nursing programs, for example.

It is assumed that you are not a mediocre student, but there are degrees of excellence; to understand where you fall on this scale, you should evaluate both the course content of your undergraduate curriculum and your grades in key courses.

It is a mistake to conclude that after college, your educational record is fixed once and for all. The fact that you have completed undergraduate work and have your B.S. or B.A. does not mean that your record cannot be improved upon by taking extension courses in subjects that will add strength to it. Bear this in mind as you read this chapter: It is never too late to enrich your undergraduate record. Just your willingness to continue your education and improve upon it will impress admissions offices, providing the work you have done is meaningful and of high quality.

Undergraduates reading this chapter may have time to alter their curriculum plans to meet the desires of graduate admissions offices. It is not necessarily sufficient to graduate with a high grade point average; graduate schools will be unimpressed if they find that you have taken courses considered to be lacking in rigor or intellectual challenge. A demanding curriculum is essential.

Here then is an outline of the academic work expected of applicants to rigorous professional and academic graduate programs.

UNDERGRADUATE CURRICULUMS
FOR PROFESSIONAL SCHOOL CANDIDATES:
MEDICINE AND ALLIED HEALTH PROGRAMS

Unlike law or business programs, which lay down no specific courses applicants must have passed, pre-med programs require ten terms of science and math — two terms each of basic chemistry, organic chemistry, biology, physics, and calculus. These should be completed by the end of junior year, the same year you take your medical aptitude tests. Good colleges make it tough to get into their pre-med programs — organic chemistry is the watershed course — and are tough about recommending those who do not do well in their pre-med courses. Falling below a 3.0 GPA in the pre-med portion of your curriculum usually means that you must make up this lackluster performance by taking additional science courses, on the grounds that some medical school will be impressed by your diligence and the breadth if not the depth of your scientific knowledge.

Some medical schools also require applicants to have taken some particular combination of English, behavioral or social sciences, and humanities courses. Brown University, for instance, requires three semesters of behavioral or social sciences, NYU three hours of English, while Dartmouth calls for no required courses other than the sciences and math cited, but assumes a well-rounded liberal arts education. Details on such requirements will be found in the invaluable volume *Medical School Admission Requirements*, published annually by the Association of American Medical Colleges.

But what about majors? No medical college specifies a required major, and the AAMC cautions against picking a major you think will enhance your admission chances, a science particularly. "Medical schools are most concerned with the overall quality and scope of undergraduate work," they say in *Medical School Admission Requirements*. Notwithstanding, 70 percent of applicants in 1984–85 entering classes chose to major in a science. The table we reproduce here should be studied carefully, for it shows that nonscience majors were just as successful in gaining admission as the science majors; those majoring in health-related technical subjects like nursing and pharmacy tended to be less successful.

We would urge those starting their college careers to consider seriously majoring in a nonscience for the breadth it will add to your education. Those few who contemplate a medical career after college without having had pre-med training should not worry that their major was economics, history, or some other nonscience. The medical and health professions need the widest variety of talents, and those who have done well in any major subject are equally strong candidates as the biology or chemistry majors.

ACCEPTANCE TO MEDICAL SCHOOL BY UNDERGRADUATE MAJOR 1984–85 ENTERING CLASS

A survey by the Association of American Medical Colleges produced the following results:

Undergraduate major	Total applicants	Percent of total	Accepted applicants	Percent of major
Biological sciences				
Biology	13,367	37.1	5,894	44.1
Microbiology	963	2.7	399	41.1
Physiology	328	0.9	142	43.3
Science (other biology)	561	1.6	332	59.2
Zoology	1,546	4.3	675	43.7
SUBTOTAL	16,765	46.6	7,442	43.4
Physical sciences				
Biochemistry	1,676	4.7	1,003	59.8
Biomedical engineering	252	0.7	157	52.3
Chemical engineering	406	1.1	243	59.9
Chemistry	3,928	10.9	2,111	53.7
Chemistry and biology	508	1.4	265	52.2
Electrical engineering	190	0.5	114	60.0
Mathematics	319	0.9	176	55.2
Natural sciences	331	0.9	168	50.8
Physics	228	0.6	137	60.1
Science (general)	225	0.6	97	43.1
SUBTOTAL	8,063	22.4	4,471	55.5
Nonscience subjects				
Anthropology	152	0.4	87	57.2
Economics	247	0.7	149	60.3
English	349	1.0	180	51.6
Foreign language	224	0.6	122	54.4
History	263	0.7	171	65.0
Philosophy	161	0.4	89	55.3

continued

continued from page 82

Political science	166	0.5	86	51.8
Psychobiology	356	1.0	196	55.1
Psychology	1,600	4.5	709	44.3
Sociology	127	0.4	52	40.9
SUBTOTAL	3,645	10.1	1,841	50.5
Other health professions				
Medical technology	399	1.1	133	33.3
Nursing	470	1.3	174	37.0
Pharmacy	443	1.2	146	33.0
SUBTOTAL	1,312	3.7	453	34.5
Mixed Disciplines				
Double major (science)	559	1.6	274	49.0
Double major (science and nonscience)	616	1.7	309	50.2
Interdisciplinary	135	0.4	78	57.8
Pre-medicine	929	2.6	448	48.2
Pre-professional	197	0.5	120	60.9
SUBTOTAL	2,436	6.8	1,229	50.5
Other*	3,723	10.4	1,758	47.2
GRAND TOTAL	35,944	100.0	17,194	47.8

*Those applicants not reporting an undergraduate major are included in "Other."
Source: *Medical School Admission Requirements 1986–87*, Association of American Medical Colleges, Washington, D.C.

What we have said about prospective medical school applicants applies in general to those contemplating dental schools, veterinarian schools, and other professions in the health sciences. Future clinical psychologists should naturally take some psychology courses, but they need not feel obligated to major in psychology. Those contemplating a public health career would do well to take courses in government, geography, economics, and sociology. Here again, admissions committees will be looking at your level of academic achievement in an effort to discern the likelihood of your success in the stiff programs of their particular schools.

In brief, there is no full prescription for getting into medical school or any school in the health sciences field. The best preparation over and above the required science and math is a broad liberal arts education. Also consider an emphasis on communication skills, of increasing importance as litigation and ethical debates put a premium on doctors' abilities to express themselves clearly and unambiguously in writing or in speech.

TWO DIFFERENT ACADEMIC RECORDS

Howard Cohen in his four years at Rutgers took twelve semesters of science, adding molecular cell biology and cell physiology to the standard list of science courses. He majored in psychology, doing a long paper senior year on Freud's conflicting views about human nature. Other electives he took were Shakespeare's tragedies, existential philosophy, economics, music appreciation, American history, and modern art. With a GPA of 3.3 he was admitted to six medical schools and chose the University of Rochester.

Laura Abbott majored in biology at Smith College. Her electives included anthropology, modern European history, Renaissance painting, the English novel, the American Constitution, and sociology. Her GPA was 3.2. Admitted to eight medical schools, she enrolled at Northwestern.

LAW SCHOOLS

"How, then, can you prepare for the challenge and rigor of legal education? . . . The key . . . is developing certain basic reading and reasoning skills." So says *The Official Guide to U.S. Law Schools*, published by the Law School Admission Council and Law School Admission Services. Reinforcing this generalization under the rubric "How to prepare for law school," the guide continues: "People who are considering law as a profession should understand . . . broad ranges of undergraduate preparation, the value of learning to think, write, and speak creatively and logically."

Supposedly those who are admitted to accredited law schools have a satisfactory capacity for reading and reasoning, yet it is disquieting to observe that only about a third of those who enter law school complete their training. Statistics compiled by the Office of the American Bar Association Consultant on Legal Education show, for example, that of 127,195 enrolled law students in 1983, only 36,389 were awarded J.D. or LL.B. degrees.

Getting into law school, then, is only the beginning. Staying the course is, for a variety of reasons, beyond the capacity or the will of two-thirds of those who start out in law school. There is no assurance that even the well-prepared law student will last the three years to a degree, for the study of law may prove boring or otherwise incompatible with the student's interests.

THE MYTH OF A PRE-LAW CURRICULUM

Some colleges do offer a pre-law curriculum. These are not recommended. Why? Because such courses merely dabble in the law and add little to the student's reading and analytical skills. "So-called 'prelaw curriculum,' " says *The Official Guide*, "is a myth, a mistaken notion based on an inexact analogy to premedical programs. . . ." *The Official Guide* continues:

"Law schools want students who can think, read, and write and who have some understanding of the forces that have shaped human experience. You can acquire these attributes in any number of college courses, whether in the humanities, the social sciences, or the natural sciences."

Many law school catalogues or bulletins offer no guidance whatever as to an appropriate undergraduate curriculum for applicants. Yet such open-endedness should not lead you to think that anything goes. Courses in photography, home economics, personal hygiene, or physical education, however personally practical, count for nothing when applying to law school.

The law school applicant should take courses in writing and literature, history and political science, and economics. It would be wise to include one of the following: accounting, statistics, or computer science (these courses can alternatively be taken after college at night, in summer school, or, if you can't fit them into your schedule, by correspondence from accredited institutions). Science courses are optional, but may be useful in that some law today relates to medical issues, environmental concerns, patent disputes, industrial accidents, and the social responsibilities associated with such issues as cloning or surrogate pregnancy.

What does this add up to in curricular terms? A smorgasbord of liberal arts courses with the major left up to the individual. The important thing is the depth and intensity of study, for almost any challenging liberal arts program is good preparation for the enormous amount of reading and case analysis that has to be done in any law school. You can major in engineering, philosophy, linguistics, math, biology, Russian literature — there really is no limit, so long as you stick to the liberal arts, and these, remember, include science.

Again, what is undesirable are undergraduate courses surveying aspects of the law, such as contracts. You can major in business and take liberal arts courses as electives. But leave the law courses to the law schools. Think of getting ready for law school as a matter of:

- learning to read critically;
- learning to write and speak clearly and forcefully;
- reaching an understanding of human institutions and values upheld by law;
- becoming a creative thinker who can bring original solutions to problems of law.

CORNELL LOOKS AT PRE-LAW STUDIES

The following advice from Cornell University Law School develops a bit more fully some of the arguments for a broad liberal arts background as preparation for studying law:

"The Cornell Law School does not prescribe a prelaw course of study. Law touches nearly every phase of human activity, and consequently there is practically no subject that can be considered of no value to the lawyer. Prelaw students should, however, be guided by certain principles when selecting college courses.

"1. Pursue personal intellectual interests. . . .
"2. Attempt to acquire or develop precision of thought. . . . Courses in English literature and composition and in public speaking may serve that purpose. Logic and mathematics develop exactness of thought. Also meriting attention are economics, history, government and sociology, because of their close relation to law and their influence on its development; ethics, because of its kinship to guiding legal principles; and philosophy because of the influence of philosophic reasoning on legal reasoning and jurisprudence. Psychology helps the lawyer understand human nature and mental behavior. Some knowledge of the principles of accounting and of the sciences . . . will prove of practical value to the lawyer in general practice.
"3. Study cultural subjects. . . ."

Admission to law school can be highly competitive, and your grades will make a big difference. To cite an extreme case, Stanford's class of 1985 had 172 members; there were 3,300 applicants. "The largest part of each class is drawn from the upper 5 percent of their undergraduate colleges, and the upper 3 percent of the LSAT pool," notes the *Stanford University Bulletin*. So many applicants misjudge the academic competition that they are up against. Doing extremely well academically is the sine qua non for admission to a great law school. But if your record suggests that you are out of the running for the likes of Stanford or a good school like Boston College, you can still improve it to the satisfaction of other excellent, less-competitive schools, by taking additional liberal arts courses either during your undergraduate career or after graduation.

THE RECOMMENDATIONS OF BOALT HALL

In the catalogue of Boalt Hall, the school of law at Berkeley, the following suggestion is made concerning pre-law study:

"Students in a position to structure their curricula might do the following: develop skills in communication, both written and verbal, and take courses in which written work is vigorously edited; develop analytical and problem-solving skills; obtain breadth in humanities and social sciences in order to understand the social context within which legal problems arise; and acquire a general understanding of economics, because a significant portion of legal problems are related to the economic functioning of the society. In selecting specific courses, consultation with an undergraduate advisor may be desirable."

LESS THAN FOUR YEARS OF COLLEGE?

It is possible to get a law degree without having a bachelor's degree. We do not recommend it. It is not that the law schools accepting such students do not provide training to pass the bar exams, but that you will subsequently be competing in a world of college graduates on uneven terms.

Why not make the effort to complete your undergraduate work? You gain nothing by not getting your degree, and you miss the course content, leadership opportunities, and the maturing influence of life on campus.

BUSINESS ADMINISTRATION PROGRAMS

Like law schools, business schools do not lay out a recommended curriculum for prospective applicants. Thus one of the attractions of an MBA is that anyone with a good solid liberal arts bachelor's degree has an excellent shot at admission to a good program. The rule of thumb, once again, is that the stronger your undergraduate record, the more prestigious the school you can and should logically apply to.

"Naturally, your academic background is the most important feature in the evaluation of your application," says the catalogue of Jesse H. Jones Graduate School of Administration, Rice University. But no suggestion is offered as to specific courses that may help to qualify you. Next to this statement is an endorsement of the school by a banker who graduated from Princeton in 1979 with a B.A. in comparative literature. Other graduates endorsing Rice's program majored in biology, history, chemical engineering, economics, and accounting.

Most MBA programs admit applicants with bachelor's degrees in anything. The important thing is not what you study but how well you do in your courses. "Our MBA Program looks for candidates whose analytical and organizational abilities, communication skills, motivation and leadership indicate potential for successful careers in professional management," says the MBA catalogue of the University of North Carolina at Chapel Hill. The average entering student had a 3.3 GPA, so you can see that academic achievement is a must for their applicants.

Here are some other comments from MBA program catalogues:

NYU: "When evaluating an academic record we consider the level of success achieved and the quality of the undergraduate programs pursued."

University of Chicago: "The School encourages applications from students in all fields of undergraduate study including the liberal arts and sciences, engineering, law, and commerce. . . . Although no specific courses are required for admission, the School recommends that students prepare themselves with the equivalent of first-year calculus. Some experience with computer manipulation is also helpful not but required. The emphasis in many of the M.B.A. courses is upon a broad set of applied analytical techniques developed for decision-making in management. This requires that students have the aptitude to learn and apply some relatively basic mathematical techniques. The program is self-contained and any additional mathematical tools can be acquired in the program."

Yale School of Management: "The 366 students in the Classes of '86 and '87 earned undergraduate degrees from over 125 colleges and universities in the United States and abroad, studying in a wide variety of fields, including economics (15%), the humanities (29%), science and mathematics (11%), engineering (15%), ·the social sciences (23%), and business or commerce (7%)."

Columbia University: "The faculty believes that solid preparation in English, history, economics, and social sciences is desirable. Adequate preparation in mathematics is essential for strong performance in the Columbia M.B.A. Program. While specific courses in mathematics are not required for admission, the Faculty strongly recommends that admitted students successfully complete an introductory calculus course prior to matriculation, either in college or in a post-college extension program at the collegiate level."

Indiana University: "Individuals with academic backgrounds in science, engineering, and liberal arts are encouraged to apply. Although the curriculum is structured to accommodate non-business undergraduates, it does assume that each student is familiar with both differential and integral calculus. . . . Admission to the Indiana University Program is highly selective . . . the current average GPA for entering students . . . is 3.35 on a 4.0 scale."

Carlson School of Management, University of Minnesota: "We welcome applications from graduates of accredited colleges and universities with a variety of majors — liberal arts, sciences, business, engineering, and other undergraduate fields. . . . Each year approximately 185 new students enter the full-time MBA program. The selection process is highly competitive — average GPA 3.30 (on a 4.0 scale)."

Washington University in St. Louis: "No prior coursework in business or management is required for admission."

We need not belabor the point about academic preparation for admission to a good MBA program. The essentials are these:

1. A bachelor's degree from an accredited college or university.
2. An undergraduate program of significance, with few nonacademic credit courses.
3. Strong undergraduate performance, preferably a GPA of 3.0 or better.
4. Demonstration in coursework of good communication skills.
5. College math, taken in college or after.
6. Strengthening of any weakness in the record by coursework taken after college.

UNDERGRADUATE CURRICULUMS FOR CANDIDATES OF OTHER GRADUATE SCHOOLS

Thus far we have been talking of academic qualifications for the big three professional programs, law, medicine and other health sciences, and business/administration. What about the entrance requirements for schools of engineering, of science, education, government, communications, architecture, and the arts?

ENGINEERING AND SCIENCE PROGRAMS

Only graduates of engineering schools or graduates with a bachelor of science degree go on for advanced degrees in these fields. The first hurdle for engineers is being admitted to a good engineering school; then they must complete the rigorous undergraduate program in a chosen field — civil engineering, chemical engineering, electrical engineering, aeronautical engineering, marine engineering, mining, or nuclear engineering. Some programs take five years and you earn both a bachelor of science and a master of science.

Anyone who gets a bachelor's in engineering needs little guidance about further academic training. Even high school students who are strong in math and science know pretty much how to go about pursuing an engineering or a science career. Some who start an undergraduate program find they are not cut out for it, but those who finish are usually qualified to do graduate work.

Admission to graduate engineering programs is often really a matter of your being recommended by faculty members to institutions where they have contacts. There is a considerable old boy network among engineers, and this is true of scientists too.

WHEN MODESTY IS NO VIRTUE

A newspaper report about a brilliant boy who won a science prize in a suburban high school for experiments on air quality in the city caught the eye of a Princeton alumnus, who contacted the student and asked him where he was going to go to college. He named a local institution with an adequate environmental studies program. He had never thought of Princeton or any selective college. His family being of modest means, he proposed to commute to college.

Finally persuaded to apply to Princeton, he was admitted, won a full scholarship, and after graduation did his graduate work at MIT. It is highly unlikely that he could have gone on to MIT from the institution he had originally wanted to attend.

The moral to this story, directed especially to high school students and their counselors, is: Aim as high as you can if you have a gift for science and engineering. Underestimating your potential early on can be embittering, as you may find yourself limited in your career because of your educational background. Modesty in such cases amounts to selling yourself short. Go for the gold!

The college science major in biology, physics, chemistry, zoology, or astronomy does not follow the kind of professional path laid out by engineering schools. Many such majors after graduating go into nonscientific fields like banking, law, and corporate management. Instead of a graduate degree in science they may opt for one of the professional degrees in law, business, or the health sciences. But those who wish to follow a research career at a university, a corporation, a foundation, or under government auspices must go on for at least a master's and more usually a doctorate in their discipline.

Here again the undergraduate faculty plays the principal role in advancing scientific careers. Science professors realize that the majority of students in a given class have no intention of doing graduate work in science. In addition to teaching, however, they wish to identify and encourage the potential future scientist, even to the point of calling a student's attention to his or her aptitude for science and stimulating an interest in a scientific career.

It should be made clear that the science student seeking faculty support will not get very far merely on charm or manipulation. Scientific accomplishment in college is quantifiable, much more so than accomplishments in the so-called soft humanities disciplines. Conversely, good scientists are not likely to be overlooked today when there is a shortage of Ph.D.s, needed to strengthen the United States in its struggle to compete economically against countries whose scientific education programs are much more supported by their governments.

It behooves the undergraduate science major today to give serious thought to any faculty suggestion to consider graduate training. The lure of immediately higher pay in business and industry is an understandable temptation. But in the long run the compensation paid to highly trained scientists is not inconsiderable. Ph.D.s in science may start out in the private sector at the same level as MBAs and lawyers.

NONSCIENCE GRADUATE PROGRAMS

Admission to academic graduate programs in fields outside of science is best achieved through a challenging liberal arts program in which the student shows a capacity for superior work. It should be remembered that in graduate school no grade less than a B is considered passing. Thus quality graduate programs are usually open only to those with a 3.0 GPA or higher. It is, moreover, easier to begin a nonscience academic program than to finish with a doctorate. Those who seek a Ph.D. are very strong students. Satisfying the requirements for a master's is within the reach of students who have not the drive or scholarly qualities needed to earn a doctoral degree.

What you major in is less important than the strength of your academic record. You can major in English literature or classics or psychology and get a master's in a history program or an economics program. A distinguished anthropologist now at Brandeis University majored in sociology in college. A professor of classics at Rutgers got a master of history degree at Columbia before getting a doctorate in classics, his undergraduate major.

Again, as with admission to science and engineering graduate programs, admission to nonscience graduate programs depends heavily on faculty recommendations. Those seeking admission to an academic graduate program immediately after graduating from college should rely heavily on faculty advisers in determining the programs to which they ought to apply.

We have a word of caution: A candidate should have a clear objective in mind, and a full awareness of the potential usefulness of the graduate degree in finding a job or in increasing a capacity such as writing or painting. The key question to ask is: How is this degree regarded outside the university (or within it for that matter)?

A case in point: A teacher of French with a Ph.D. in that subject was unable to get any job other than that of part-time language teacher at the university where she earned the degree. In such jobs the rate of pay is about one-fourth that of full-time faculty, and you cannot participate in the health or pension programs of the university. After a few years, with no progress in sight, she gave up the job and became a docent in a local museum. This is not an isolated incident. Many universities, for budgetary reasons, exploit Ph.D.s and those with master's degrees in this way.

To avoid disappointment after earning a graduate degree in an academic field, try to make sure in advance that your hard work will have a satisfactory payoff. This may require seeking out several of those who hold a graduate degree from the program that interests you and asking them for frank assessments of the program's value.

IT'S THE DEGREE, NOT THE COLLEGE, THAT COUNTS

How often we hear bright high school seniors assert that they are applying to colleges that will assure them of admission to the best graduate schools. It is a fundamental mistake to say that any college degree by itself is an assurance of admission anywhere. All you need do to prove this to yourself is look at the list of colleges represented by their graduates in the graduate classes of prestigious institutions. You will find, if you take the trouble to count them, that the students often come from over 200 different colleges. "Last year's entering class represented 236 colleges and universities," says the 1988 Georgetown Law Center admissions brochure.

Of course the Ivies are more heavily represented than most schools, and those with a Georgetown bachelor's degree make up a fourth of the first-year law students. But this only suggests that graduating from prestigious colleges may improve your chances of admission to a prestigious graduate school, not guarantee it.

Another problem almost never mentioned by either students or educators is that it is much more difficult to attain an impressive academic record in a prestigious college than elsewhere. An honors prep school graduate at Harvard complained: "It's almost impossible to get an A here." He therefore did not even apply to a Harvard graduate program. He went to Fordham to study philosophy. Had he gone to Fordham as an undergraduate and gotten straight A's, he might well have been admitted to a philosophy Ph.D. program at Harvard.

We want to emphasize the point we have been making all along: Graduate schools want the best students from whatever institution they attend.

WAYS TO BEAT THE COMPETITION

Given the large numbers of strong liberal arts graduates, how does the good student assure himself or herself of admission to a meaningful graduate program, aside from getting as many A's as possible? Answer: Look for an academic specialty that is attractive to graduate schools, one that most students for one reason or another avoid, such as:

- Languages — If you are fluent in a foreign language, you have an edge on the competition applying to many graduate schools. As the globe shrinks, so to speak, the ability to speak another language will be of enormous value in business and government. Because you will probably be offered a good job, the graduate school will more readily admit you.

  One way to become fluent in a foreign language is to arrange to spend a couple of years in a foreign country after graduating from college. There are jobs available, and a company agreeing to hire you may well pay to send you on to graduate school.

- International affairs — This usually involves a reading knowledge of one or more foreign languages but not necessarily fluency. The job opportunities in international organizations for those with specialized knowledge are many. Again, graduate schools are looking for people they can place.
- Communications — There is a premium placed on the ability to express yourself clearly in writing and in spoken presentation. Any encouragement you get as an undergraduate on your written work is a sign that you may be talented in this regard and should think of adding some communications study to your curriculum — courses in journalism, writing, public speaking, possibly a course in the nature of media. You might later combine graduate study of communications with a specialty in business or any number of fields.
- Computer science — You need not be a math major to do well in computer programming or related subjects. This capability is valuable in almost any field today. Thus a prospective historian with computer expertise may be more attractive to a graduate school than a competing applicant without it.
- Combined undergraduate majors — An athlete instead of taking the traditional physical education major might combine it with economics with an eye to a job with a sports equipment company and later an MBA. One woman as an undergraduate combined Russian language with child care, then went on for a Ph.D. in child psychology and is now an expert in Soviet child care.

With a little imagination you can discover all sorts of ways of standing out without necessarily being the most brilliant member of your class. Put together a decent academic record with some specialty like photography, using it to illustrate papers or a thesis. An education major who is also a good actor can strengthen his or her record by taking drama courses and subsequently making a case to a graduate education program that acting experience will be useful in teaching — and not necessarily in teaching drama.

Beating the competition academically then may be a matter of creative thinking, or even of, to use a phrase educators don't like, marketing yourself, by showing admissions officers that you have something special to offer.

Step Four Checklist

1. Examine your undergraduate experience in light of expectations of particular graduate programs.

2. If you discover any weaknesses, consider improving your record by taking courses now to strengthen it.

3. Remember that pre-med students need not major in science, that there is no such thing as a pre-law curriculum, that you can major in anything and be admitted to an MBA program.

4. In applying to engineering school, rely on undergraduate faculty to steer you to the right program.

5. Nonscience academic graduate programs are usually open only to students with high grade point averages. Admission to programs at the master's level is easier than admission to doctoral programs.

6. Develop some specialty or pluses such as a language skill or computer literacy that make graduate programs want you.

STEP FIVE

Prepare for Graduate College Tests

THE IMPORTANCE OF THE TESTS

The scene is familiar, even banal, yet dreaded: a classroomful of human beings frantically filling in little boxes or circles for three to as many as six long hours. They are not high school students doing their College Boards, but grown men and women, twenty to eighty years old, taking graduate school admission tests against the clock: the Graduate Management Admission Test (GMAT); the Graduate Record Examination (GRE); the Law School Admission Test (LSAT); the Medical College Admission Test (MCAT), and the Dental Admission Test (DAT).

Scores on these tests provide admissions committees with vital criteria by which to judge applicants' suitability for graduate work. To be sure, other criteria guide admission decisions — grade point averages, recommendations, nonacademic accomplishments, the quest for ethnic, gender, and geographic class diversity — but mediocre or poor test scores can cast an enormous shadow on a candidate's file. Moreover, candidates for academic programs seeking certain fellowships must submit their GRE scores.

It is hard, therefore, to overemphasize the importance to graduate school candidates of spending many hours over several weeks preparing for graduate tests. The well-prepared do well at test time. They have done their homework, taking a number of past tests against the clock for practice by themselves, scoring the tests, studying the results. They have become familiar with the kinds of questions to expect and are used to the time constraints of the tests and the pressures imposed.

When you prepare intelligently you discover your weaknesses and can drill to overcome them. Mistakes made on the verbal sections of a test suggest the need for vocabulary drills and a review of grammar — Harvard science majors in one survey showed a loss of verbal skills by senior year because of their tendency to report lab work in a kind of shorthand code. Candidates taking tests with math questions (the GRE, GMAT, MCAT, and DAT) may need to review fundamental mathematical concepts, rules, and operations unless thoroughly familiar with them. Many law school candidates must improve their reading habits before taking the LSAT.

The amount of time needed for test preparation will depend on the individual; fifty hours might be sufficient for a student still in college, while twice that might be needed for the average candidate who has been out of college for several years.

The Official Guide to U.S. Law Schools in discussing preparation for the LSAT puts the issue well:

"It is impossible to know when an individual has prepared enough, but very few can achieve their full potential by not preparing at all." The same can be said for the GMAT, the GRE, the DAT, and the MCAT.

THE IMPORTANCE OF TEST PREPARATION

Stanley Kaplan, head of the oldest and largest tutoring service for graduate school candidates, says his students sometimes spend as little as thirty hours in classes, but are welcome to spend up to two hundred fifty hours repeating classes and listening to tapes. No one has ever put in two hundred fifty hours at Kaplan's, but one nervous woman, after testing poorly on her first actual LSAT, was so determined to overcome her weaknesses that she spent two hundred hours at a Kaplan tutoring center. For her pains she got a phenomenal 48 out of 50.

Neither Kaplan nor anyone else can guarantee anyone a particular score. You could put in two hundred hours and get a score that would make you think you had wasted too much time preparing for the test. But then you might have done worse without the work. As one of Kaplan's administrators told us, "You can't come here for weeks without improving your test-taking ability."

Note that phrase: test-taking ability. Some people of considerable intelligence do badly on tests simply because of lack of familiarity with the test format. Smart as you are, you haven't time when the clock is running against you during an actual test to puzzle out the way questions must be answered, to scratch your head and think, "What do they want?" Only those who know from practicing on tests what the examiners want can expect to do well. This is the nature of these tests.

And you can't say you weren't warned by the examiners themselves. *The GRE Bulletin of Information* tells anyone taking this test:

"Data on the General Test show that scores often rise as a result of taking the test more than once. Scores of some examinees do decline. By making use of the General Test in this Bulletin, you may be able to derive the benefit of this practice effect. After you have familiarized yourself with the sample questions, take the practice test under conditions that simulate those in an actual test administration. Be sure to observe the time limits imposed and focus your attention on the questions with the same seriousness as you would if taking the test to earn scores. Later, go through the practice test again, identifying the category of each question and reviewing the paragraphs that pertain to that type of question."

So you are told to prepare. And this is not all. The bulletin goes on to inform you that you can obtain no less than six tests given in the last two years. And there are test-taking strategies presented for study in the bulletin. Given the length of the tests being simulated, it is easy to see how you could put in thirty hours just taking practice tests and reviewing questions.

HOW PREPARATION PAYS OFF

In this step you will learn something about the nature of the tests and why we urge you to undertake the considerable task of preparing rigorously for

---

TRICK QUESTION

Here is a trick math question from the GMAT:

Determine whether you have sufficient data to solve the problem below. Choose answer

A if statement 1 alone is sufficient but statement 2 is not

B if statement 2 alone is sufficient but statement 1 is not

C if both statements 1 and 2 together are sufficient but neither statement alone is sufficient

D if either statement alone is sufficient

E if neither statement alone nor both statements together are sufficient

What is the average weight of five men?
1. The total weight of three men is 480 lb
2. The total weight of two men is 260 lb

The answer is E.

You cannot assume that the weight of all five men is 740 pounds, because the same men might have been counted twice, once in each group. To answer the question using both statements (C), statement 2 would have to read: "The other or the remaining two men weighed 260 pounds."

The only way to prepare for a zinger like this is to do a number of tests. Familiarity with the kinds of questions to expect on graduate admission tests sharpens your aptitude for answering questions by getting you in the habit of looking at a question more closely. Test taking is itself an acquired skill.

them if you are seeking admission to the better graduate programs. The reward for the work we propose should be a good test score and also a good start on the academic road you choose to follow. Prepping for tests stretches the mind and helps get you in mental shape not just for the tests but for the formidable demands graduate school will make on you.

THE RATIONALE BEHIND THE TESTS

Why another round of tests? Isn't a bachelor's degree sufficient evidence of capability to do graduate work? No, because the difference in the training at a highly selective state university like Virginia and that at a marginal college is so vast that no admissions committee can measure the comparative merits of candidates from such different institutions. Without national tests, selectivity of admissions would have to be achieved by admitting only top students from schools well known to admissions committees. The rationale for graduate tests is thus the same as that for the SAT, which came into being after World War II, when thousands of high schools began sending students to college for the first time. Admissions offices were faced with the impossible task of distinguishing well-prepared from inadequately prepared students trained in schools they did not know. The SAT provided a benchmark, enabling admissions committees to compare hordes of students academically in an objective fashion. Thus the good student from a country high school scoring in the 1200s in math and verbal tests could be predicted to be a better freshman academic prospect than a good Phillips Exeter Academy student scoring in the 1100s.

As graduate school applications expanded dramatically after Sputnik (1957), administrators of graduate tests began to adopt the same format as that of the College Board's famous SAT; the exams are made up of multiple-choice questions that test verbal skills, math skills, and/or knowledge of course content. In fact, both the GMAT and GRE are administered by the same organization that developed the SAT, the Educational Testing Service in Princeton, New Jersey, test administrator for the College Board. The LSAT, MCAT, and DAT have separate administrations: The LSAT is administered by the Law School Admission Council/Law School Admission Services in Newtown, Pennsylvania, the MCAT by the American College Testing Program in Iowa City, Iowa, under contract to the Association of American Medical Colleges, the DAT by the American Dental Association.

Each of these five graduate tests is designed for distinctly different admissions committees. The GMAT tests aptitude for studying business and administrative work; the GRE tests aptitude for studying academic subjects in graduate school. They both include verbal and math questions. The LSAT tests aptitude for studying law and has no math questions. The MCAT and DAT test aptitude for studying first-year medical and dental school courses. In addition to verbal and math questions (called reading skills analysis and quantitative analysis), there are MCAT questions that test knowledge of biology, chemistry, and physics subject matter and the ability to solve problems in these three sciences. DAT questions test knowledge of biology, chemistry, and organic chemistry.

Academic graduate programs requiring thorough knowledge of a particular subject ask candidates to take one of the GRE subject tests offered in seventeen fields: biology, chemistry, computer science, economics, education, engineering, French, geology, history, literature in English, mathematics, music, physics, political science, psychology, sociology, and Spanish.

If you are bright and well prepared, you can do well on these tests, not necessarily just on one but on two or more, should you wish to add to your professional capabilities. A practicing lawyer who passed the LSAT years ago may later want to go to business school. He or she will then take the GMAT. In this case, of course, separate test preparation will be necessary.

We trust that graduate school applicants will not concern themselves at this point with the educators' controversy over the value of testing as a measure of intelligence or academic potential. A very few schools have dropped the test requirement (Harvard Business School no longer requires the GMAT, nor does Johns Hopkins Medical School require the MCAT), but their applicants are such achievers that their transcripts usually speak adequately for themselves. Institutions that drop the tests tacitly acknowledge that tests are unpopular, even painful for the best students, and that they are of dubious value in assessing the brightest students. Given several hundred academically outstanding applicants, admissions committees at highly selective schools have to judge them on the basis of other qualities — proven leadership capacity, communication skills, evidence of integrity, manual dexterity in the case of potential surgeons (athletic ability can be a factor in such a candidate's favor), clarity of purpose — and by other means — interviews, essays, and faculty recommendations. But in making decisions among hundreds or thousands of good but less-than-outstanding applicants, most admissions committees find that test scores taken together with grade point averages are critical.

WHAT THE MCAT MEANS TO THE MEDICAL SCHOOLS

Here is how the Association of American Medical Colleges describes the usefulness of the MCAT:

"The MCAT provides medical school admission committees with a nationally standardized measure which enables schools to compare applicants with widely different personal and academic backgrounds. The test has been carefully designed and constructed so that individual scores will have the same meaning from year to year, making possible direct comparisons of applicants who have taken the test at different times."

Hence the anxiety in that classroom full of adults being tested once again like schoolchildren. For they are competing against thousands taking the same test in centers all over the United States. Anxiety is not in itself a bad thing when alloyed with confidence. The two may seem contradictory, but just as the best actors suffer momentary stage fright, so the most prepared applicant cannot help but fear that a trick question or a careless mistake may be his or her undoing.

Thus, the motto to paste on your mirror is: PREPARE! PREPARE! While the subject matter differs, the principles of preparation are the same for any graduate admission test: sharpen your verbal, reading, and (for all but the LSAT) your math skills and sharpen your test-taking skills in general. In addition, because GRE subject tests are best taken soon after finishing courses in the subject, it may be necessary for someone who has been out of college for a time to repeat a survey course to prepare for such a test.

WAYS TO PREP FOR ANY GRADUATE ADMISSION TEST

As noted, preparing for a graduate admission test is essentially a matter of becoming so acquainted with the nature of the questions you will be asked that they no longer make you nervous. First, you should get hold of one of the following official publications appropriate to your field:

The GMAT Bulletin of Information
The GRE Bulletin of Information
The Official Guide to U.S. Law Schools: Prelaw Handbook
The Medical School Admission Requirements
DAT Preparation Materials

The GMAT and GRE bulletins are published by Educational Testing Service and distributed free to college counseling offices. They can also be obtained by writing the Educational Testing Service (ETS).

For the GMAT bulletin write:
   Graduate Management Admission Test
   Educational Testing Service
   CN 6108
   Princeton, NJ 08541-6108

For the GRE bulletin, write:
   Graduate Record Examinations
   Educational Testing Service
   CN 6004
   Princeton, NJ 08541-6004
(Note that the two addresses are distinguished only by different CN numbers.)

The GMAT Bulletin of Information provides just about all you will need to know about the test: its nature, fees ($26), the four test dates in October, January, March, and June, procedures for taking the test, how to prepare for the GMAT, tips on test-taking and guessing, how the test is scored, the location of test centers, and thirty-nine sample test questions. Three complete tests are available in *The Official Guide for GMAT Review*, for which an order form is provided in the bulletin. It is well worth the $9.95 to get these tests for practicing.

The GRE Bulletin of Information provides similar general information about the tests, but in addition there is a description of each of the seventeen subject tests, as well as a complete sample test with answers that allows you to practice. An order form is provided for the purchase of the *GRE General Test* booklet, containing three sample tests at $7. Practice tests in the seventeen subjects are available at $6 each.

The Official Guide to U.S. Law Schools: Prelaw Handbook is published annually by the Law School Admission Council/Law School Admission Services. College counseling offices have copies, as do public libraries; you can buy it for $14. In it you will find an invitation to write LSAC/LSAS for *The Law Package*, a free bulletin that includes descriptive material about the LSAT and a tryout LSAT. In *The Official LSAT Sample Test Book* are three additional sample tests, for which the charge is $14; fifteen more sample tests are available at $5 each.

The handbook can be ordered from:
Publications
LSAC/LSAS Dept. 0-6
P.O. Box 63
Newtown, PA 18940

The Law Package and *The Official LSAT Sample Test Book* may be had by writing to:
LSAC/LSAS
P.O. Box 500-57
Newtown, PA 18940

The Medical School Admission Requirements is published annually by the Association of American Medical Colleges of the United States and Canada, and is widely available in colleges and libraries, but relatively inexpensive to buy at $7.50. Write:
Association of American Medical Colleges
Attn: Membership and Publication Orders
Suite 200
One Dupont Circle, N.W.
Washington, DC 20036

It contains only a summary description of the MCAT, so in addition candidates should write to the same address for the *MCAT Student Manual*, which also costs $7. The manual describes the MCAT in detail and provides a sample test. It also outlines science topics to be assessed in the science problems of the test and describes the reasoning and decision-making skills to be tested. It describes types of materials on which test questions are based, and specific mathematics preparation needed by students.

DAT Preparation Materials is available to dental school applicants free. Simply write to:

Division of Educational Measurements
American Dental Association
211 East Chicago Avenue
Chicago, IL 60611

Samples of four DAT examinations may be obtained for $2 from the same address. The samples come in a 28-page booklet with answers at the back. A foreword explains that "There are no short-cuts to the process of learning and this booklet is not designed to provide the applicant with an opportunity to by-pass the extensive process of absorbing basic information through class participation and months of study."

Candidates seeking more information about the DAT, particularly the science test, should consult the book *Admission Requirements of U.S. and Canadian Dental Schools*, available in libraries and counseling offices. It can also be purchased for $18.50. Write to:

American Association of Dental Schools
1625 Massachusetts Avenue
Washington, DC 20036

If a college or university in your area offers special classes to prepare you for graduate tests, by all means try to attend them. Costs are usually modest, and the classes force you to keep to a schedule that is often difficult to maintain on your own. Or you can go to a tutoring school such as a Stanley H. Kaplan Education Center (they are located in thirty-four states) at an approximate cost of $500 to $600. The popularity of Kaplan's centers says something about their usefulness: of the 130,000 who attend annually, 40 percent are graduate school candidates, as compared with 30 percent being tutored for the SAT (the remaining 30 percent are being tutored for licensing exams). With a growth rate of 10 percent a year, Kaplan's must be doing something right, though even they will guarantee nothing.

The Stanley H. Kaplan Educational Center is the largest tutoring school, but in every metropolitan area you will find either a university that offers tutoring courses, or professional tutors who compete with Kaplan. The best way to find these places is to look at the education sections of the metropolitan dailies, where tutoring schools advertise.

If there is no tutoring school in your area, or you find the cost too burdensome, and you must prepare on your own, here's a summary of the steps to take:

A GOOD TUTORING SCHOOL DESERVES
YOUR CONSIDERATION

We encourage applicants to graduate programs who can afford tutoring to go to a school if there is one in their area. Tutoring for graduate tests makes sense in most cases, whereas tutoring for the SAT is only occasionally wise. The College Board has long disparaged SAT tutoring courses as a waste of time and money. The Educational Counseling Center has been cautious in sending students to such courses, for while they can be helpful in raising scores, a high school student who has done mediocre work in school often has difficulty doing the work tutoring schools demand. In such cases test scores are unlikely to improve.

For those applying to graduate programs, the case is different. Tutoring is helpful because it trains the applicant in test-taking. College graduates have already read enormously, and most have math skills. What they need is not more reading or fundamental math lessons, but drilling in the kinds of questions to expect, and help in disciplining themselves to handle each test block in the time allotted. Graduate tests are more sophisticated than the SAT, and the verbal/math components are unlike tests you take in college, which test your knowledge of subject matter based on courses you have completed. A tutoring school in effect gives you a course in graduate admission test-taking. For those who have been out of college awhile tutoring is especially valuable in rebuilding confidence and giving you back a feel for hard academic work.

1. Study the latest ETS GMAT or GRE bulletins, LSAT and MCAT handbooks, or *DAT Preparation Materials*.
2. Buy the requisite practice tests and/or a test guide like Barron's.
3. Again, the best preparation for subject tests is a semester or more of coursework in the test subject.
4. Draw up a realistic test study schedule and then systematically follow it. This is difficult. Like dieting it takes self-discipline. But you must do it in order to compete against those who are preparing with all due diligence. How much time should you allow yourself for such a self-taught course in test-taking? The average student will benefit from eight to ten hours a week over the course of six to eight weeks. Just taking one practice test requires three, four, or six hours; the test must be scored and the results studied to find your weak points; then you must work to overcome weaknesses — in grammar, in calculation, in science problem-solving, in analytical reasoning, evaluation of facts, knowledge of a subject. The American Dental Association suggests that you allow two to three months to prepare for the DAT.

At Kaplan's a course consists of eight five-hour sessions, or forty hours in class, which includes test-taking time. Students are urged to spend an equal number of hours on out-of-class drilling. That's eighty hours. Our proposal for a self-taught course calls for forty to eighty hours of preparation. This is not overkill by any means. For college students taking tests during junior or senior year this means integrating prepping for tests into a heavy schedule of classes, labs, and outside assignments.

Here is a one schedule form that will allow you to note your progress in test-taking:

Test to Be Taken--------------

Week	Time spent on test	Time spent reviewing and drilling	Score
1			
2			
3			
4			

(et cetera)

When taking a test you must replicate test conditions, using an alarm clock if possible, or another person to signal the end of a test section. Do not take part of a test and return to it later. This is self-defeating, because you are not rehearsing the exact conditions of the test, which is a continuous process. You cannot leave the room during a test. It is therefore absolutely imperative that you assure yourself of an uninterrupted three, four, or eight hours (the MCAT allows you an hour and a half for lunch).

What you get from all the work is relative mastery of test-taking, and this does not mean learning gimmicks; it means learning to use your reading ability more sharply and to use your powers of mathematical reasoning so that you can respond more quickly to questions, sharpening your sense of logic, deepening your knowledge of required subjects.

THE NATURE OF THE TEST QUESTIONS

Each graduate admission test has its own formulation for testing you. Here's a brief summary:

The GRE is designed to measure verbal, quantitative, and analytical abilities. Questions are grouped in seven thirty-minute sessions. You cannot go back to a section once it is over. There are nine types of questions: analogies, antonyms, sentence completions, arithmetic, algebra, geometry, data interpretation, analytical ability, and analytical reasoning. It is scored on a scale of 200 to 800. You are penalized for wrong answers, so guessing is not advised. There is no penalty for not answering a question.

The GMAT measures verbal and mathematical skills that have been developed over many years of schooling. There are eight separately timed sections in this four-hour test, but there are only five types of questions: analysis of situations, reading comprehension, sentence correction, data sufficiency, and problem-solving. The total score scale is 200 to 800. As in the GRE, wrong answers count against you, unanswered questions do not.

The LSAT measures a range of mental abilities related to the study of law. It consists of six thirty-five-minute sections plus a thirty-minute Writing Sample. (The Writing Sample is not scored but is sent for evaluation to each law school to which the candidate applies.) There are four types of questions: logical reasoning, reading comprehension, analytical reasoning, and evaluation of facts. The range of scores is 10 to 50, with no penalty for wrong answers, so guessing is advised; all questions should be answered no matter what the uncertainty.

The MCAT measures specific scientific knowledge as well as verbal and quantitative skills. It consists of two sessions, morning and afternoon, with two sections of questions in each session. Science knowledge and science problems are given in the morning; skills analysis: reading, and skills analysis: quantitative in the afternoon. In addition, at the end of the morning session there is a forty-five-minute session devoted to writing an essay that is not scored but sent to certain admissions committees as part of a pilot project for evaluation. The test is designed so that almost everyone is able to finish each section without undue pressure. Each section is scored on a scale of 1 to 15. Less than 8 is a poor score for a section.

The DAT is comparable to the MCAT, but in addition to measuring aptitude for dentistry study, it measures manual dexterity. Four sets of questions require half a day to administer. They test science knowledge, reading comprehension, quantitative ability, and perceptual ability (two- and three-dimension problem-solving). Scoring is on a 1 to 9 scale.

SOME TEST-TAKING TIPS

1. TIME
   - Get a good night's rest before the test. Do not cram.
   - Arrive half an hour before the test, and make sure you allow for possible transportation delays. Bring a watch.
   - Take time to read all test directions carefully, even though you will be familiar with them from taking sample tests.
   - Never hurry through a question. Do not skip and skim. Haste makes waste.
   - Plan the time you will spend on each section.
   - If you finish a section ahead of time, go back and review your answers. Do not look ahead to another section.
   - Answer time-consuming questions after you have answered those you can do quickly.

2. MARKING
   - Use a No. 2 soft lead pencil. Bring three or more and an eraser.
   - Fill in the box on the answer sheet completely when you are sure you want to indicate that box. If you change your mind, erase it completely. Never mark more than one box per question, for this will count against you.
   - After skipping a question deliberately, double check to see that subsequent marking is in the proper box. In other words, watch out for putting the right answer in the wrong box.

TAKING THE ACTUAL TEST

It should go without saying that you must keep track of all the particulars about when tests are given, when you must register, how much they cost, where you must take them, what they consist of, what time they begin, how long they last, and what you need to bring to the test. Here is a checklist, for example, for the GMAT:

- When — Tests are given four times a year: in October, January, March, and June.
- Registration — Closes a month prior to the test, but you should register well in advance to insure that you get your choice of center and to allow time for correcting anything amiss in the application.
- Where — Test centers in all states, Puerto Rico, Guam and the Virgin Islands, as well as in 104 countries abroad are listed in the ETS bulletins.
- Cost — $28.
- Time — 8:30 A.M.
- Duration of test — Four hours.
- Identification needed — Bring admission ticket plus an ID with photo (student ID, driver's license, employee ID, or passport). Note: credit cards, social security cards, and draft cards are not accepted as valid identification.
- What to bring — Three or four No. 2 soft lead pencils and a watch. Calculators, books, and scratch paper are not allowed to be brought into the test room.

CONSIDER THE TESTS AS A NEW EXPERIENCE

Much of what we have said here may seem elementary, but thousands of those taking graduate admission tests perform below their capability because of failure to prepare for them meticulously. Attention to detail is one requirement of those pursuing graduate study. Simple mistakes made by a doctor can mean disaster. A lawyer's slip can ruin a client.

Look upon tests, therefore, as a new experience for which you must get ready. You are on stage giving a command performance. You cannot afford to goof. Overconfidence is no more helpful than uncertainty. This is a time for measured evaluation of your capacity. As important as it may be to know subject matter, calculation skills, and vocabulary, it is equally important to know how to take one of these tests.

This is not something you are trained for; you have had no long buildup of experience with tests like these. Your willingness to acknowledge your ignorance of graduate testing should lead to the requisite preparation for your test.

Step Five Checklist

1. You must prepare for graduate tests (the GMAT, GRE, LSAT, MCAT, DAT). Few do well who don't.
2. Familiarize yourself with the nature of a test by taking practice tests, available in bookstores or by mail order. Practice tests with an alarm clock. Don't fudge.
3. Keep a record of practice tests taken and note the time spent studying.
4. Consider attending a tutoring school. Over 150,000 applicants do so every year.
5. Spend forty to eighty hours preparing for a test. That's what your competition will be doing.

Write Strong Personal Statements

THE SIGNIFICANCE OF PERSONAL STATEMENTS

An applicant to graduate school is usually asked to include with the application one or more personal statements, each consisting of a few paragraphs stating motivations for graduate study, plans after graduating, aspirations, interests, accomplishments, or anything else that seems relevant to an admissions decision. Sometimes an admissions committee wants your personal reaction to a proposal they offer you — how you would react to an employee's refusal to do something you asked, for example. What could be more disarming than an invitation to talk about the most important person in the world, yourself, or to give a personal reaction to a trying situation?

Yet the best of us choke at such an opportunity and wonder, after writing something: Is this what they want? A natural reaction, but one that is obviously counterproductive if allowed to dominate your thinking as you compose the statement.

Just what members of an admissions committee want is to a certain extent impossible to know, since they are strangers to you. Of some of their expectations, however, you can be sure. No law professor, doctor, or Ph.D. going through candidates' folders is saying things like, "Hasn't told us about his childhood," or "Hasn't said why she went to college so far from home," or "Doesn't even mention honors courses," or "Why not say how much he expects to make as a dentist?" Nor are these busy, astute men and women looking for the kind of essay you wrote when applying to college. But if they are not looking for anything in particular, how can you ever write something that will make an iota of difference to your acceptance or rejection?

Put yourself in the chair of an admissions committee member for a moment and consider the task to be carried out: reading the personal statements of several dozen candidates who have already been screened as possible admits. They all have high GPAs and good test scores, but as many as half of them must be rejected. How can personal statements help an experienced faculty member (most graduate admissions committees are made up of faculty or administrators who have been professors) decide whether to vote for or against?

WHAT HARVARD BUSINESS SCHOOL WANTS

Here are the questions requiring extended written answers, personal statements of varying length, in the 1988 Harvard Business School application:

1. What evidence can you present to demonstrate your capacity to perform well academically in the Harvard MBA Program?
2. Describe your avocations and hobbies.
3. Describe an ethical dilemma you have experienced. Discuss how you managed the situation.
4. Given your experience with your current employer and given the opportunity to effect one change, what would that be? How would you implement the change?
5. Describe your three most substantial accomplishments and explain why you view them as such.
6. What factors led you to decide that graduate education in business administration would be most helpful to your career development?
7. Discuss the vocations or professions, other than administration, which you may have considered.
8. Which of your character traits do you consider your strengths? Which would you most like to change or improve?
9. Describe a situation or job in which you felt you had some responsibility and tell us what you learned from that experience.

MARTIN BURDICK'S CASE

Let's look at the example of Martin Burdick, an MBA candidate, some of whose personal statements are presented below. With a very mediocre 2.70 GPA at the University of Virginia and a very high GMAT score, he managed to be accepted at Columbia, Cornell, Wharton, and UCLA. Harvard and Tuck (Dartmouth) turned him down.

Martin is the son of the owner of a substantial hardware firm. His father holds a Harvard MBA. There was no problem about Martin's prospective career, but he wondered how effective and influential he would be in his father's business. Using the Harvard questions as a basis for self-examination, he began with rough drafts, worked to improve them, and ultimately was able to prepare very cogent personal state-

continued

continued from page 109

ments. Take the subject of his weak academic record:

"I graduated from Virginia with a BA in history. That event remains the highlight of my undergraduate career. Instead of studying hard, I hardly studied. This sentiment was borne out in my GPA — a lofty 2.7, a remarkably mediocre achievement accomplished chiefly through long hours of neglect. Instead of concentrating on my schoolwork I managed to indulge myself in everything from scuba diving to heavy option stock trading. Though I was successful at these, my grades suffered."

With this off his chest Martin then wrote a lengthy description of his work experience. It began:

"Upon graduating from college I started work in the family business and experienced a remarkable turnabout in both attitude and confidence. I suspect the reason for this change was a combination of maturity, fear, and my having an opportunity to focus my energies and achieve concrete goals. In any event I am proud of my accomplishments in business and I am keenly aware that I still have much to achieve."

He then described in detail his experience in the company, how he learned BASIC, COBOL/CICS programming and rose to head a staff of twenty-five programmers and analysts in one year. Next he described his solution to a problem of expanding inventories: "I put together a core team of eight, representing operations, research, purchasing, distribution and DP/MIS. . . . After a few months it became clear that inventory was swelling due to inaccurate demand forecasts and sharp increases in speculative buying. . . . We constructed a sophisticated inventory management system that produced more accurate demand forecasts. . . . The project was so successful that we are now considering packaging the results for sale. . . ."

An additional personal statement described how he got the Young Leadership award in 1985 from the Society for a Better Community for his work in helping open nineteen new independent stores with strong minority participation.

Finally, why an MBA? "For me an MBA is of great importance in determining the future of our business, which must expand, but how? Through acquisition? Or should we diversify into a different industry like typewriter manufacturing? And how will we finance expansion, through a public offering or borrowing? I am eager to acquire the tools to help answer these questions by means of an MBA."

A confident, happy young man comes through in these personal statements, which helped get committees to overlook his poor college record.

One of the positive side effects of the personal statement is that writing it clarifies your own ideas and feelings about a graduate program. It forces you to examine your motives in light of your record, and if it is an honest self-evaluation, you will benefit from it.

VERONICA'S CASE

A second example illustrating the critical nature of personal statements is that of Veronica Evans. At the insistence of a guidance counselor she rewrote her essay four times. She had quite a story to tell. In eighth grade she learned she had Turner's syndrome, which is a chromosomal disorder that limits physical growth to five feet or less, and prevents a woman from having children. Her GPA of 3.12 at Northwestern is commendable but not brilliant, and her MCAT score of 64 is not exceptional. Yet she was admitted to six good medical schools including NYU and Boston University. She is currently at the University of Rochester's excellent medical school. Her deeply moving essay made a difference. We present it in part:

"When I found out I had Turner's syndrome, I ran. I disassociated myself from the situation and attempted to run my life as if nothing had happened. This was not possible. In preparing for medical school I have discovered the ability to face consequences and found channels for change.

"I have not only formed relationships with people, but have also become able to talk to my family. I now have the ability to express what I have gone through. . . . As I began to experience relationships with people, I realized that for me science will be an indispensable tool, a method which I can use to do something about the things I care about most.

"In this past year I have discovered areas that not only interest me, but that I can devote my life to. I work on turtle brain cells in an attempt to establish a connection between two types of neurons. . . ."

In this essay Veronica honestly conveys her original dismay at discovering her tragic illness and how she overcame self-pity by making a commitment to a scientific usefulness to humanity. The contrast between her rather average academic performance and her intense convictions is striking.

A LAW SCHOOL STATEMENT

The case of Eric Holman is also instructive. He was an A and B student at Duke, and scored 38 on the LSAT; that meant stiff competition for admission to such law schools as those of Cornell and Columbia. Here is some of the personal statement that helped him:

"During the 1984 fall term and the following two summers, I interned

continued

continued from page 111

for a New Jersey assemblyman, researching and drafting legislation on shareholder protection, the right to counsel, loitering, videotaped wills, armed robbery, and government access to casino computer records. The legislation that I take the most pride in drafting is an act concerning employees who work as telecommuters (they work at home and contact an office by telecommuting equipment). The bill requires that they be paid at the same rate as those in the office.

"To write it I talked to many telecommuters and others in the field. The bill is expected to influence other legislatures. My analytical and writing skills improved a great deal under the close scrutiny of the assemblyman. . . . I hope to run for legislative office and write bills after finishing law school. . . ."

This statement gives an admissions committee the impression of an earnest, hardworking young man, who already has some legal experience, and who could profit from legal training and make any law school proud to have trained him.

Eric was not an outstanding student at Duke and his 38 on the LSAT was only average. Yet he was admitted to Penn, Vanderbilt, UCLA, and three other law schools, and wait-listed at Columbia, Cornell, and Chicago. He is now at the University of Pennsylvania.

You will note that nothing is said about grading personal statements. All judgments are subjective and no grades are ever given. Some members of the admissions committee may be more impressed by a personal statement than others. When there is considerable disagreement about a personal statement, other criteria become more important in determining an admission decision.

THERE ARE MANY MARGINAL CANDIDATES

We present the three good but not outstanding students above as typical of many graduate school applicants. In a sense all applicants are marginal. Every year Harvard, Stanford, Princeton, MIT, and the other top schools turn down outstanding candidates whom they would probably have admitted to another class when the competition was less severe. Looking at the numbers — academic record and test scores — places many graduate school candidates in the category called Possible Admit by Princeton when evaluating folders of potential first-year students. Hence the importance of the personal statement. It may just turn the tide for any applicant to any good graduate school.

That is why we ask you to devote more attention to the personal statement or required essay than you might otherwise think necessary. Writing is not easy even for professional writers, who spend as much time or more rewriting their texts as they do on a first draft. You are not asked to compete with masters like Henry David Thoreau, Annie Dillard, or John Updike. But graduate schools expect you to be able to write clearly, logically, and with a modicum of grace and imagination. If you already have this capability, then Step Six will not require much of your time. But if you have any doubts about your writing skills, our suggestions combined with practice can help you to improve. Strangely enough, the more you write, the better your writing becomes and the easier it is to say on paper what you have in mind.

ESSAYS FOR GRADUATE SCHOOL DIFFER FROM COLLEGE ADMISSIONS ESSAYS

When you applied to college, the essay that went out with your applications was an attempt to bowl over the admissions offices with your individuality. You tried to show your uniqueness by writing up some unusual experience. If you were creative, you let that come out in humor, eloquence, graceful and poetic expression. You also tried to show you would fit into campus activities and sports, and how you would be a constructive force in college. Your essay was designed to demonstrate what you could offer to the institution.

Yes, in a similar sense your extracurricular achievements in college can look good on your graduate school application, but to build an essay around them will work only if they are related to what you plan to do after you have a graduate degree. Being captain of the baseball team is an unlikely basis for a personal statement. Having nearly or entirely completed college and perhaps already having a job or holding down an internship, you are a mature individual. Your personal statement must therefore reflect this maturity and show how your record and accomplishments have led to personal growth. Admissions committees look for evidence of such development for the reason that it suggests that you are capable of further development under their tutelage. The personal statement can, in this sense, be helpful in projecting the future of a candidate: Will he or she be a good or a great doctor, lawyer, teacher, editor, captain of industry, government expert, economist, et cetera?

An account of your junior year abroad is of no interest to a medical school admissions committee if you do not relate it to your prospective career. The fact that you have organized a rock group cannot by itself make an MBA committee sit up and take notice as it would an undergraduate admissions office. Again, you have to show somehow that this accomplishment bears on your career — thus the rock group experience can show a talent for organizing, making money, managing people, promoting yourself, and possibly for going into the entertainment business if this is your bent. As another example, your mastery of a foreign language equips you for work in a multinational company.

Cleverness in a personal statement is counterindicated. What opened the eyes of bored professional readers of college applicant folders only annoys men and women professors who screen applicants without pay in the hopes of finding new students they would like to teach.

Finally, the college admissions officer is a generalist seeking to admit a number of different academic types to satisfy all the academic departments of his school. In one essay he may spot a future ecologist and in another a banker. The graduate school admissions committee person is a comparative Johnny-one-note, looking for new students for the one or few programs of that school. He or she is extremely focused. The best personal statement in applying to graduate school is one that says in effect: I will be a credit to this graduate school both while attending and in my career afterward.

REVISE, REVISE, REVISE

College students seldom are required to rewrite their papers in the interest of improving the text. Their manuscripts come back to them marked with comments like "not clear," "inconsistent," "poorly organized," "weak expression," "punctuation," "spelling," "subjective," "not true." Such corrections usually will not have much impact, especially if the grade is disappointing. The paper is filed and forgotten. The corrections, instead of being a learning experience, are likely to be taken as an annoyance, or an insult. And if the paper is graded "A" without comment about weaknesses in the writing, the student naturally has no way of knowing that he could improve his expression.

Learning to write clear English is like learning to play the piano: it takes practice, and you must go over a piece of prose until it is reasonably smooth. This means redrafting, which is tedious but essential.

WORK ON THE LEAD

But what should be rewritten? Two things to aim for in a personal statement are (1) an arresting, attention-getting lead sentence or paragraph, and (2) clarity of expression.

Let's take the lead. In a society so exposed to media, you are competing for the admissions committee's attention with newspapers, magazines, and sprightly ad copy. We expect all writing to be immediately rewarding. Our boredom threshold is low indeed.

Here's how the Associated Press started a story of an unusual woman: "Colina, Chile — Leontina Albina does not expect much from her children on Mother's Day. She did not raise the 53 of them to be like that."

A *Boston Globe* story started this way: "San Francisco — Last January there were bad vibes in the Haight-Ashbury neighborhood here. The merchants and residents were fed up with the trash and litter caused by transients. The Summer of Love had chilled into the Winter of Discontent."

You can similarly pep up personal statements by deliberately avoiding the obvious opener: "I first wanted to be a doctor when I went with my father on his hospital rounds." Instead why not use:

" 'Can't you reduce the pain, doctor?' the young man asked. 'Not without side effects that will complicate your recovery,' the doctor replied. This was my first exposure to the hard side of medicine. When as a high school boy I saw my gentle father refuse to sedate a patient after a gall bladder operation, I thought to myself, 'I want to be as gutsy as Dad. I want to be a surgeon too.' "

An MBA candidate got his personal statement off to a lively start in this fashion: "You can't know what you don't know. That's why I think I need an MBA. Last year I had to throw in the sponge and file for bankruptcy. I don't want this ever to happen again. For me an MBA is going to be a form of preventive business medicine."

An applicant to several top journalism schools opened her personal statements with: "Five years on a metropolitan daily have taught me one thing: I need time to develop skills I simply can't learn on the job. You can't expect busy editors to drop everything to coach your reporting or analyze weaknesses in your copy."

These are not brilliant ideas, but they beat "I want an MBA in order to learn the accounting procedures necessary for an entrepreneurial success." Or, "After five years as a member of the working press it's time for me to take a year off to polish my journalistic skills."

You too can write a good lead by abandoning the chronological account and searching for something significant in a sequence of observations you plan to present to the committee. Ask yourself: What's important in what I am going to say?, rather than, When in time should I begin my statement? Thus if you are proud of earning a Phi Beta Kappa key, you do not begin with a history of all the A's you earned, you begin with the moment you learned you had been invited to join that illustrious fraternity of scholars.

You can easily develop this habit of noticing how reporters do this in the newspapers or on television. They seldom respect chronology except in adjunct, sidebar material. They report first that the Iranian Airbus was shot down with a loss of 290 passengers, not that the crew of the *Vincennes* spotted something on the radar, hesitated briefly, then fired. That follows. The lead, the headline present a few significant facts with little regard for chronology.

AIMING FOR CLEAR EXPRESSION

The second thing to be conscious of in your revision is making sense of everything you write. Will your thought be clear to someone else? You know what you have in mind, but there's many a slip between a thought and its expression. A good guide to clear expression is *The Elements of Style* by William Strunk, Jr., and E. B. White, the famous *New Yorker* writer and the author of *Charlotte's Web*. It's also a good idea to show your copy to someone else for comment. When you hear that something is not clear, correct it, clarify, clarify, clarify.

A CONCLUDING PERSONAL STATEMENT

We conclude with the following example of a good personal statement, written by someone admitted to the School of Social Work at the University of Wisconsin:

"My early childhood in Mississippi, where I lived until the age of eleven, was characterized by domestic tension brought on by my father's weaknesses — he was a poor farmer, drank too much, and quarreled frequently with my mother. As a result I grew very close to my mother, sympathetic to her struggle to keep her family going through menial work, and I listened to her hopes that I would become a doctor someday. After her divorce and remarriage when I was ten, we moved to Wisconsin, where my stepfather became a modestly successful salesman of printing services. I excelled in high school and was determined to become an obstetrician. My mother had become a practical nurse and continued to encourage my medical ambitions.

"But things did not work out exactly as planned. I was admitted to Oberlin College, and freshman year I got into a first-aid class. This is when I began having doubts about becoming a doctor. Among other things, I was trained to counsel students on the abuse of drugs and alcohol, as well as on overeating, and I had some success in helping a few addicts in the city during vacation. At the same time some negative experiences with overbearing and selfish doctors gave me further pause about a medical career.

"My parents were disturbed by my change of heart, but I myself felt relieved, because I knew that my future lay in helping people the way my mother had helped me in childhood, by caring. I began to study psychology and sociology and one of my professors introduced me to the career of social work. As I progressed through college with good grades, my mother became more understanding of what I was preparing for — a career of social service.

"I know I need to do graduate work to complete my training that will allow me to work with and help individuals, families, and groups of people. Meantime, I have a job in a halfway house that I enjoy. I believe that in time I will be able to make a significant contribution to the lives of many unhappy people."

Step Six Checklist

1. Recognize the importance of personal statements in applying to competitive graduate schools.

2. Do not rely only on the kind of originality required on your college entrance applications.

3. Use the Harvard Business School essay questions as a means of practicing revealing personal statements.

4. Work on the lead sentence or paragraph after studying leads used by journalists.

5. Aim for clear expression.

6. Rewrite your statements, show them to someone for comment, and polish them to complete this important step.

Make Your Nonacademic Experience Meaningful

THE VALUE OF EXPERIENCE

"Discuss your professional objectives, both short and long range, and how your past experiences have contributed to the definition of those objectives. Be as specific as possible about the kind of positions you seek." — NYU MBA application form.

Aaron Loring at twenty-six felt that he was ready to profit from an MBA program such as NYU offers. He had performed erratically at Vanderbilt as an engineering student — twice being on academic probation, then finishing with a 3.2 GPA junior and senior year. Given that he had to compete against others who had maintained 3.2 averages for four years, his prospects for admission to a competitive MBA program would not have been good had he applied immediately upon graduating.

So he did a number of other things. He took a full-time job with a small telecommunications machinery manufacturer in Newark, New Jersey, where he had clerked during summer vacations, and was made export sales manager and then purchasing agent. While working, he took courses in calculus at Rutgers and computer programming at Fairleigh Dickinson University, and studied conversational French at the Inlingua School of Languages in Princeton.

At the end of two years he went to France and joined the sales department of a telecommunications firm there for a year, while taking a course in French civilization at the Sorbonne. A year later found him in London working for a financial organization in a training program. He was now convinced that he wanted to make a career in the international marketing of telecommunications equipment.

In response to the application question above, he concluded:

"The knowledge acquired from the variety of activities I have described on this application has progressively helped to define my professional objectives, which, in the long term, relate to the international marketing of equipment within the telecommunications industry, an industry that continues to be dominated by engineering thought. Such acquired knowledge has also made me better appreciate my short-term goal, which centers upon a structured education in management. It is this appreciation, together with the confidence with which I can state my long-term objective, that drives me at this point in time toward seeking such an education, a quality education, which I know to be fully obtainable at NYU."

Aaron is currently at NYU. And why not? He showed that he could come back from weak scholastic work, that he was committed to continued study in fields that absorbed his interest, that he could gain fluency in a foreign language, and could make some progress as a young man in the competitive world of international business. Professors teaching management love this kind of student, one who has had practical experience and has a defined career goal. They know Aaron will have no trouble landing a good job with an international company, and that he will be a credit to NYU.

Other graduate schools also appreciate the value of meaningful experience. Engineers who have worked in factories, science majors with commercial laboratory experience, communications majors with journalism experience have a strong appeal to graduate admissions committees. Why? Because graduate school is in a sense just another part of the real world of practical striving and trying to get along with people. Experience usually brings with it flexibility, a capacity for rolling with the punches and for dealing with setbacks, for accepting criticism. These character traits are helpful when you go through rigorous graduate training.

Aaron's case is a good example of how focused experience can determine a career objective. Compare it to the case of a very bright Harvard graduate with an M.A. in English who has been teaching for a number of years and suddenly finds himself financially pinched. "I'm thinking of getting an MBA," he said to us recently. Well, we told him, he might get into some kind of unimpressive program that was looking for students, but he really needed some experience in management to make academic work in a respectable university accessible and useful to him.

"But I thought that the MBA would land me a management job," he said. Not necessarily. Why would anyone pay him a good salary simply because of two years of graduate school when he had absolutely no experience save teaching English? (The idea that a graduate degree in itself will land you a well-paying job is a false conclusion reached from a superficial reading of the reports of starting salaries for MBAs that appear regularly in the media. What the statistics don't tell you is how much experience these graduates have already had, or what the quality of their degree is.)

To work first and then go to certain kinds of graduate schools is now increasingly common. It is not a vital factor in admission decisions of M.D. programs and Ph.D. programs in the arts and sciences. But it is particularly appreciated by admissions committees of MBA programs. And while many law schools are filled with college graduates who have not held any significant jobs, some law schools would like you to have some experience in the so-called real world.

The School of Law at the University of Texas at Austin concludes its application form with this request: "Describe any significant vocational, non-vocational or extracurricular activities, other experiences or other aspects of your background which you believe relate to the admissions criteria described above and which you feel the Admissions Committee should consider in evaluating your application."

Says Cornell University Law School's announcements bulletin: "Many factors enter into an admission decision. . . . Thus the admissions committee may give considerable weight to work experience. . . ."

Other things being equal, the candidate with a record of meaningful experience outside college will often be chosen over the person who lacks much exposure to the kinds of situations professional schools exist to prepare you for. This is so because, in contradistinction to undergraduate training, training in fields like law, journalism, and social work is highly professional in orientation, directly related to activity outside the university, activity that is part of the machinery of society.

THE CHANGING APPLICANT POOLS

Applicants with good college records are usually startled when they are rejected by graduate schools they think should admit them because of their academic aptitude. Laura Corley majored in English at Beloit College and graduated in the upper fourth of her class. Her extracurricular activities were largely in music — glee club, a rock group — and she spent her summers teaching sailing on Lake Michigan. A record of comparable academic achievement and extracurricular involvement would be sufficient for admission to a good undergraduate college but not to a top law school. Laura was rejected by the law schools of Northwestern, Michigan, Columbia, George Washington University, the University of Wisconsin, the University of Minnesota, and Penn.

The Law School Admission Council/Law School Admission Services' handbook, *The Right Law School for You*, quotes a law school catalogue describing what the school looks for in an applicant's record: "Typical life experiences cover a variety of endeavors, professional and otherwise, including college teaching, computer programming, medicine, film making, Olympic athletics, nuclear physics, the Peace Corps, and VISTA."

It was suggested that Laura build up a stronger record of life experiences. First, she stopped teaching sailing and got into racing competition, winning a number of races and being named her club's sailor of the year. Second, she enrolled in a community college paralegal program and became a paralegal in a Milwaukee law firm. After two years, her firm offered to help pay for her legal training, and she had no trouble this time in getting into the law schools of the University of Minnesota, the University of Washington, and the University of Southern California, finally enrolling at Minnesota.

What Laura had encountered was today's stiffer competition for places in the better law schools. Graduate applicant pools are changing in the same way the undergraduate applicant pool is changing: There are more good students competing for a relatively stable number of openings in the more prestigious, more popular schools. Undergraduate colleges that once were considered safeties now can pick and choose their freshmen from among the upper ranks of high school students. And what is true at the freshman level is becoming true at the graduate level.

In these circumstances, admissions committees feel that the more mature and experienced candidate has a better understanding of the profession, and is more aware of what he or she is getting into. Such a candidate is usually more motivated, is focused on realistic objectives, and has more seriousness of purpose.

And so life experience can count heavily in some cases as a criterion for acceptance. It is a general axiom that the more professionally related experience a candidate has had, the less significance will be given to his or her test scores and college record — in that order. We underline this as one of the most important changes that has occurred in graduate school admissions policies in the last decade. The traditional complaint of the leaders of America that higher education is too theoretical, too ivory tower, has been acknowledged. Many experienced applicants are swelling graduate applicant pools, and their accomplishments are being considered as strong evidence of their capability for serious graduate work.

THE VARIETIES OF LIFE EXPERIENCE

We have cited one basic and desirable situation, that in which applicants in their twenties had held jobs or pursued activities that are meaningful because they display the desired characteristics of maturity and motivation. There is a second common situation, that of the student who is still in college and who wants to go to graduate school right after graduating. Obviously such a student cannot have had full-time employment unless he or she has taken time off from college. Even so, this student, short of being an academic whiz, can and must demonstrate accomplishments that are evidence of talent, character, leadership, self-confidence, and an ability to handle responsibility.

The outstanding student with a 4.0 GPA and high test scores will usually be admitted to better graduate schools on academic merit alone. But most applicants have a 3.2 GPA or less, and less-than-exceptional test scores. When committees look at a number of comparable applicants, all deserving of admission to a graduate school with a limited number of places, to decide who will be accepted they closely examine the nonacademic record to see how the candidate has functioned in settings unrelated to the classroom. This record can be broken into two parts: (1) campus activities, including sports, and (2) off-campus activities pursued during vacations. Campus activities, to have weight with graduate admissions committees, must be significant; mere membership in an organization is unimpressive, but if you have been in the glee club several years and traveled widely with it, you can justifiably call this an activity you took seriously. A long list of organizations to which you managed to belong may give the unfavorable impression that you are an indiscriminate joiner, unless, like one successful MBA applicant to Northwestern, you can show that your widespread contacts made it possible for you to be a top salesman of campus services. In sports you should be a letter-winner, a captain, a record-holder; in other activities you should be a leader or top performer — star of the dramatic club, editor of the paper or yearbook (or at least among the top few editors), manager of a team, head of a fund drive, director of promotion for homecoming.

What you have accomplished away from college on a job or internship can help secure your admission to a well-rated graduate school if you can show how it relates to your graduate plans. Being a counselor in a summer camp may have helped you to understand human nature and taught you how to handle difficult communal situations, and thus led, as in the case of one young woman we know, to a decision to do graduate work in psychology.

A junior of average achievement at the University of Alabama, wanting to study law at the University of Texas at Austin, managed to get a job as a uniformed security person in a bank for the summer. His ability to relate this low-paying work to his conception of the legal issues involved in the surveillance of bank customers — should a bank be allowed to photograph customers at an automatic teller machine? — was probably decisive in his being admitted to the law school of his choice.

An urban affairs major at the University of Southern California wanted to get a master's degree in journalism. She had no journalism experience until the summer of her junior year, when she got a job as a copy girl on a Los Angeles suburban daily. This led to the occasional assignment during her senior year to help reporters run down information for stories on community affairs. She presented her case to several journalism schools, arguing for acceptance on the basis of both her strong academic record and her modest journalism experience, and enrolled after graduation at the University of Missouri School of Journalism.

In Seattle a senior at the University of Washington joined a group of volunteers who drive cancer patients to hospitals for therapy. In applying to a number of graduate schools of social work, he reported that this experience had convinced him of the importance of the attitudes of those with whom such patients come in daily contact. You must always give the sick a sense of hope, he said, and he described the case of a patient who had broken down after a wealthy driver had spoken condescendingly to her. As a result, he had devised a subtle questionnaire to help screen out volunteers who might not empathize sufficiently with the patients. He described his experience convincingly to admissions committees and enrolled at the School of Social Work at the University of Chicago.

If you still have time to pack in some summer experience before applying for admission to a graduate program, as an intern or trainee in a position related to your field of interest, by all means arrange to do so.

Another option for liberal arts students is to work with a faculty member on some project, even as a volunteer. A senior majoring in education at the University of New Mexico joined an Earthwatch expedition to San Miguel de Allende in Mexico, working with a professor of archaeology to unearth pre-colonial ruins. In his application to Columbia Teachers College he stated that this exhilarating experience would be useful to him as a grade school teacher. Many school programs now begin teaching prehistory to children in the first and second grades. He planned, he said, to show his classes his slides of the work done in Mexico, to explain how evidence of the earliest civilizations is found and used to create theories about them, and he added that he was going on other Earthwatch archaeological expeditions. He was admitted.

MAKING THE MOST OF SUMMERS

Working summers is the "in" thing for college students, not so much for earning money, as for getting acquainted with a field they think they might like to enter, be it business, government, research, religion, or education.

"There is a growing trend toward career-related summer internships," Sandra Schocket was quoted as saying in the *New York Times* in 1985, "as students increasingly worry about getting an edge that will help them obtain a good job or admission to graduate school." Schocket is assistant director of placement at New Jersey Institute of Technology.

Companies with large internship programs, like Xerox and American Telephone and Telegraph, often hire as summer interns those who have just graduated from college. Xerox reports that interns get a chance to "see if the company culture is right." An applicant to a business school can make a more convincing case for his admission by including a description of such an internship in the application.

Undergraduates destined for law school can help their admission chances by interning at a law firm or in a legislative office. Pre-med students often become summer interns in hospitals. The main usefulness of interning lies in the impact it can make on career choices. Graduate schools are impressed when an applicant can state career goals based on internship experience. A possible additional dividend is the academic

continued

continued from page 123
credit you may get from your college for your summer's work. At Bates College in Maine the political science department has been known to give credit to students interning on election campaign staffs.

For more information on internships write:

National Society for Internships and Experiential Education
122 St. Mary's Street
Raleigh, NC 27605

HOW INTERNING PAID OFF

In the summer between junior and senior year at Reed College, Mark Ascher, who had a combined major of economics and international relations, got an internship in Sidney, Australia, in the investment division of an international bank. When he started his internship, he was not certain about pursuing a career in banking; he was thinking of doing graduate work in economics and eventually getting a job in federal or state government. A widely read student who kept up with current events through publications like the *Economist*, Mark also was recognized as a good writer on technical subjects.

Mark hit it off so well at the bank that he was promised a job there on graduation at a salary of $40,000! That changed his mind about getting a graduate degree in economics. On the strength of this encouraging prospect, he took a course in finance his senior year and wrote three papers related to international banking.

After two years in Australia, Mark was transferred to London to work in currency trading. The bank advised him to apply to several good MBA programs — Wharton, Columbia, Chicago, and London University — with the assurance that he could remain on the payroll while studying full-time and thus be subsidized, since his salary was generous enough to meet tuition and living costs of $25,000 a year.

The bank provided two strong letters of recommendation (they are confidential, so their contents are not known outside the bank), and no doubt these helped Mark to be accepted at all but Chicago. Mark has decided to study in London in order to be able to continue part-time work at the bank. He is currently studying Spanish in anticipation of transfer eventually to Spain and later Latin America.

"The internship completely changed my life plans," Mark says.

Liberal arts majors should note that what helped Mark get started was the combination of subjects he was majoring in: economics, and international affairs, with its courses in political science and government.

WHERE TO FIND SUMMER OPPORTUNITIES

For undergraduates the best source of information about summer jobs and internships is your college career center. If your college is weak in this respect, then you must turn to family contacts and community resources. Competition for good openings is severe, so colleges often ask alumni to provide volunteer summer jobs and internships limited to undergraduates of their alma mater. A certain amount of imagination and aggressiveness may be needed to land a meaningful summer experience.

We should add that easily found, well-paying jobs in fields like construction, for example, may add little to your record unless you can relate the work to your desired career. A prospective civil engineer might make a good case for the usefulness of working on a road-building gang.

FURTHER EXAMPLES OF USEFUL EXPERIENCE

If you are applying to graduate school and wondering what constitutes good practical experience, here are some examples from the files of the Educational Consulting Center (some proper names have been altered to protect privacy):

- Assima Cabanis, Athens, Greece: Work experience — shareholder in family shipping business in which she had participated actively since 1981. Trainee, summer 1983, at Willis & Sons, Limited (shipping brokers), London. Trainee, summer 1984, at E. F. Hutton, London. Career objective is to manage family shipping business some day. Admitted to MBA programs of Georgetown, Vanderbilt, BC, and Babson, where she is enrolled.
- Catherine Stein, Hewlett, Long Island: Work experience — pie maker in a small-town bakery, "au pair" in France, clerk in a New York law firm reviewing hiring procedures for a corporation that had been charged with unfairness toward minorities and women, interviewing clients in a public-interest law firm, teacher of dance/theater in a ghetto school in Cambridge. Career objective to become a partner in a small New York law firm. Wait-listed by Harvard Law, enrolled in NYU Law School.

continued

continued from page 125
• Orim Sarash-Pal, Scarsdale, NY: Work experience — intern for his congressman, who wrote: ". . . a valuable and capable asset to my office, and I recommend him highly for any professional or academic endeavor whatsoever." Career objective is to work for Assyrian independence (his family left Iran after the revolution there). Admitted to law schools of Columbia, NYU, Cornell, Chicago, and Georgetown.

WRITING UP YOUR EXPERIENCE PERSUASIVELY

It might seem that experience speaks for itself, but admissions committees have no time to spend inferring the worth of what you have done. They must be told in convincing statements what your experience has been, what you have made of it, and how it will relate (a) to your graduate work and (b) to your career. Writing up an account of your jobs, internships, hobbies, and relevant extracurricular accomplishments is a critical part of the graduate school application procedure.

Just look at the rather sketchy and not easily read preliminary profile of Wilson Larkin, candidate for a graduate degree in industrial psychology, and then compare it to what he wrote about himself on his applications.

Wilson G. Larkin

"University of Connecticut, B.S., class of 1985, majored in psychology. Weak marks in math, science.

"GRE verbal 480, quantitative 610, analytical 86 percent.

"Research experience: 'Chronic Amphetamine Treatment: effect on behavior and local cerebral glucose utilization,' a paper written with faculty under grant from a pharmaceutical company, later published in *Neuroscience Abstracts*. We conducted experiments to replicate a 1978 study on the exhibition of paranoid schizophrenic behavior by rats. Significant results were found in activity and local cerebral glucose utilization. Also wrote a study of burnout in pre-hospital emergency medical care as it affects the volunteer EMT. Two burnout inventories were administered and correlated with the MMPID. Results to be submitted for publication.

"Experience:

"Mt. Auburn Hospital, Cambridge, Mass. June 1986–September 1987.

"Medical Communicator. Relayed complicated medical instructions verbatim. Maintained radio and telephone contact with police and first aid. Served at central communication facility for part of city during disasters.

"Groton Volunteer Ambulance, 1983–1986.

"Emergency Medical Technician.

"JFK Medical Center, Edison, N.J. 1979–1983.

"Junior Volunteer Day Chairman. Won competition to supervise and schedule junior volunteers throughout various departments of hospital."

Here is how Larkin turned the facts of his experience into a moving and convincing statement:

"Since the age of twelve I have been very interested in the field of medicine. During high school I put in well over 1,500 hours volunteering at my local hospital. When I arrived at college, I simply maintained my high level of extracurricular involvement, volunteering for various ambulance services and different student government organizations.

"My long hospital-based career enabled me to interact and communicate with many different people under many different conditions. The human mind began to fascinate me to such an extent that, although being pre-med, I had no doubt that I would major in psychology. Throughout my first two years, although doing well in my psychology courses, I struggled with my pre-med courses. Physiology was one of the few pre-med courses in which I excelled. This was due to the knowledge I had gained from working in various departments of the hospital. I someday hoped to combine my two interests in psychology and medicine by working in such fields as psychotherapy and drug treatment of mental problems.

"At the end of my sophomore year, I realized that I was having academic problems and that they could not continue if I planned to further my professional goals. Over that summer, although I completed my last pre-med requirement of physics, I decided that medical school was not where I really wanted to be. Throughout my ongoing hospital work I had always been interested and involved in the management of the hospital and was able to experience firsthand many different kinds of management styles and techniques. I was able to witness and experience many 'cause and effect' relationships regarding management decisions. I saw how stress and poor management can create poor morale and a work environment that is not conducive to productivity.

"I began to realize that I could combine my interest and ability in psychology with my interest and broad experience in the health-care delivery system. This realization soon turned into a passion and my grades dramatically jumped to a 3.3 and climbed higher to a 3.68 at the end of my junior year.

"Throughout the last semester of my junior year, and continuing into my senior year, I have been involved in research. During my physiological psychology course I was a researcher in a study that was published in *Neuroscience Abstracts*. I have been able to integrate my ambulance involvement into my research. A lot of research has been generated recently regarding burnout in the health-care professions. However, research subjects almost always have been nurses. The pre-hospital health-care system can be just as, if not more, stressful than in-hospital care. I decided to study burnout in one of the largest work forces in pre-hospital emergency medical care, that of the volunteer emergency medical technician, a group of which I am one. This study gave me great experience and a point to expand upon in future studies. I plan to continue my research in my last semester as well as throughout my graduate education.

"I feel that this experience will enable me to expand my knowledge in this area, as well as enable me to continue to enjoy the methodological aspects of the experimental method in psychology. Once I attain my ultimate goal of a Ph.D. in industrial/organizational psychology, I hope to continue my research while being a consultant, specializing in the area of health-care administration."

This applicant was admitted to graduate programs in industrial and managerial psychology at Columbia, Rensselaer, NYU, and the Stevens Institute in Hoboken, New Jersey.

His statement does several things for an admissions committee: It tells them that his passion for helping people is undiminished by his failures in critical pre-med subjects, emphasizes that his study of burnout among volunteer emergency workers is original, and shows evidence of his ability to put to good use things he does know. It also shows commitment and a sense of direction derived from concrete, practical experience.

Larkin is an object lesson to anyone who despairs of achieving his graduate school goals. Learn from failure and from experience where your future lies; don't fight city hall. If you are not a science or math whiz, find out what you are good at. Be flexible; it's a sign of maturity. Stubbornly pursuing a direction in which you consistently stumble is a sign not of persistence, but of unwillingness to stand back and admit that you have chosen the wrong path. It is interesting to note that the former chairman of the management consulting firm Arthur D. Little, Lieutenant General James W. Gavin, washed out as an Air Force pilot but went on to become a paratrooper and became the dashing commander of the 82nd Airborne Division, leading the first American paratroopers into Normandy on D-Day in World War II.

SUMMING UP THE EXPERIENCE STEP

Nonacademic experience has become an increasingly important criterion in graduate schools' admissions decisions. Since your objective is not to be admitted to just any graduate school, but always to aim for admission to the best possible program for your level of performance, you should do two things:

- Engage, during college or after, in nonacademic activities, whether jobs, trainee positions, internships, pro-bono volunteer work, or extracurricular activities and sports, that can be related to your career objectives.
- Write about your experience in such a way as to convince a committee

looking at your record that you are mature and focused in your career goals.

A dramatic indicator that experience means much to admissions committees is their willingness to admit older applicants who for years have been out of the habit of doing academic work. "We know they must struggle with the books at the beginning," one MBA dean has said, "but their long habits of problem solving and responsible decision making allow them to respond more quickly and surely than their more academically acclimated younger peers."

There was a day when the scholastic academy was removed from the "real world," but that passed away with the call by the Franklin D. Roosevelt administration to professors to implement the New Deal. This involvement of university faculty in practical affairs of government, diplomacy, and business broadened during and after World War II. Professors, serving on graduate admissions committees, do indeed know the real world, and they expect as much of you.

Step Seven Checklist

1. Relate your work experience to your graduate aims. It must be perceived as fostering meaningful personal development by an admissions committee.

2. If you lack work experience, spend a year or two getting it. Develop an extracurricular record late in college if necessary.

3. Your work experience can compensate for lackluster grades and test scores, so make your achievements on the job or as an intern clear to admissions committees.

4. While in college make the most of summer vacations with jobs or internships or volunteer projects. Even if you are only sailing or playing tennis, do competition sailing, get into tennis tournaments.

5. In your application to a graduate program, write about your work experience with enthusiasm; show how important it has been to you in setting career goals.

STEP EIGHT

Market Your Strengths

THE SELF-MARKETING CONCEPT IN ADMISSIONS

In *Scaling the Ivy Wall* we wrote that "self-marketing is the great neglected step" in the college admissions process. We can say this with even more emphasis about applications to graduate school. Marketing brings seller and buyer together, you, the applicant, being the seller, and the graduate school being the buyer. We use these commercial terms metaphorically to underscore the fact that you ought to "sell yourself" to the right graduate program, make the committee want you to enroll. This does not mean using hyperbole or in any way misrepresenting yourself. It does mean putting your best foot forward and letting the light shine on your strengths.

An example of self-marketing came to our attention recently. A woman persuaded Boston University Medical School to allow her to study for her degree part-time, and did not complete her studies for seven years (the usual time is four years).

Susan Filene at thirty-nine was raising her two sons when she talked to the BU administration about their policy of allowing special students to pursue "alternative pathways" to a medical degree. She said she needed to continue working part-time with her husband renovating property, but wished to enroll as a medical student. Her argument was persuasive.

"I found the BU Medical School faculty to be very sensitive to my personal requirements," she says. "I think what I have done creates something of a model for more women to manage medical school on their own terms. I never felt that I was waiting to start my life. I lived my life fully as a medical student." She is now interning at a Boston hospital on a part-time basis and has applied to another hospital for admission to a program in psychiatry.

BU rarely accepts part-time medical students. Some medical schools never do. Susan Filene found the program that might admit her and sold the admissions committee on her ability to complete the work.

You cannot accomplish what this ambitious woman has done without impressing the administration with your capabilities. Yet there are hundreds and even thousands of openings in graduate programs for the right people. If you feel you are right for a particular school, let them know, make them feel your enthusiasm and hunger for what it has to offer you.

BU will still tell you that you must be a full-time resident to study at its medical school, but a person who has strengths that appeal to the school can cause rules to be bent. This is an extreme case, but we cite it to persuade you to set aside all preconceptions when it comes time to make your case as an applicant.

DON'T BE OVERLY MODEST

We say market your strengths. In applying to graduate school, neither reticence nor unassuming modesty is appropriate. Soon after hearing that Columbia University was starting a master's program in real estate, Brad Huntley came to the Educational Consulting Center for advice on getting into that program. His academic record at the State University of New York was not exceptional, and neither were his GMAT scores, but he was an outstanding student leader — president of his class, of the student council, and of his fraternity. In college he showed entrepreneurial talent by starting a laundry service that netted enough money to allow him to invest in local real estate. By graduation he owned $400,000 worth of commercial buildings.

At the age of thirty he was now a successful salesman of commercial properties for an Albany realtor. He also carried on civic activities in Junior Achievement, introducing high school students to business concepts and the principles of free enterprise.

In helping assess his strengths, his counselor urged him to write about his sensitivity to the needs of local communities and their fear of the bad impact of commercial real estate development. He could cite examples of provisions for playgrounds and affordable housing that had helped win approval of his projects.

"You will be competing with a lot of New York City hot shots," he was told, "but Columbia does not want a monolithic group of students, all with the same background. What you lack in exceptional academic allure, you make up in specialized knowledge few other candidates will probably have."

To make the point that Brad could add to Columbia's program by bringing to the classroom his experience in dealing with the boards of small communities, it was suggested that he recapitulate his experience in six one-page summaries of real estate deals he had arranged, each requiring the solution of some special local problem. These summaries had the merits of brevity and readability. Furthermore, they were full of human interest.

Brad also requested an interview, saying he wished to find out whether he would make a suitable candidate for Columbia's new program. During the interview he probed assertively, without being aggressive, and at the conclusion he announced that he now knew that Columbia could do remarkable things for his career and that he would send in his application shortly. He told the committee he also planned to apply for admission to real estate programs offered by MIT and Wharton. Subsequently he was one of only forty students admitted in 1987 to this outstanding Columbia real estate management program.

MAKING A CLASS PIE CHART

What Brad did was to make use of the class pie chart concept. Put simply, every class in graduate school is made up of a diverse student body: The better schools are national in character and wish their enrollments to reflect the diversity of the nation; this means they seek as large a percentage as possible of women and minorities, for example, some foreign students, a representation of diverse undergraduate institutions, good geographical diversity, and students with something special to offer. Thus, other things being equal, minorities and women have a graduate admissions edge, as do applicants from regions remote from the school, because fewer of them apply. And so too with the student who brings some unique personal experience to a program.

Brad's strength was his experience in selling commercial real estate in a regional market. In this respect he faced little competition. A pie chart of his chances would look like the one on the opposite page.

Brad learned that he was the only applicant with a regional background in real estate. This made him unique and suggested that, other things being equal, he had a good chance of acceptance.

When you believe that you face strong competition for admission, one thing to do is to see if there is something about you that makes you exceptional among a number of candidate look-alikes. Study a class profile and conceive of the class as a pie chart, divided into appropriate slices, such as 30 percent women, 10 percent minorities, 5 percent foreign, 15 percent geographically remote, with the remaining 40 percent constituting the competitive average. If you fall into the last category, your chances are reduced by the sheer number of candidates who qualify on these grounds for admission to a class with a limited number of places. Your challenge then is to present your particular strength or strengths in such a way that you stand out from the crowd. By making pie charts based on the class profiles of the graduate schools which you are considering applying to, you will be able to see into what slices of each pie you fit. The smaller the slice you're in, the better your chances of acceptance.

BRAD'S PIE CHART

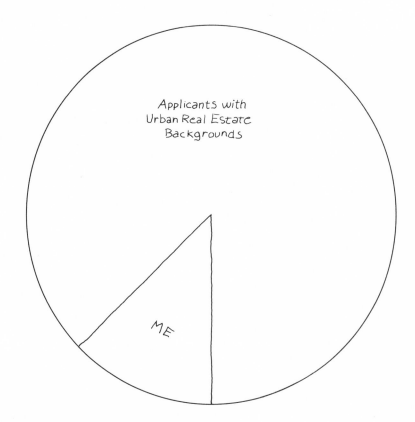

Applicants with
Urban Real Estate
Backgrounds

ME

THE SPECIALTIES PIE SLICE

In slicing up a class pie, you may find a small specialty slice you can fit into. For example, business schools are under pressure to admit more applicants who will go into manufacturing or into nonprofit work. By making your intention known about such careers, you may add to your chances of admission.

Applicants to medical school who express a keen desire to work in rural or blighted areas are often more attractive to admissions committees than others with similar qualifications who intend to stay in big cities.

Applicants to any graduate program with foreign language fluency or with an international background should conceive of this as defining a possible pie slice. This is especially true for business school applicants, but can be extended to those who want to do graduate work in government, law, medicine, and other disciplines. The multinational corporation is now so common that one large executive search firm says that 30 percent of the requests it receives are for high-level executives with some international experience.

As you examine a graduate program, look for the specialties within it and evaluate them as possible niches for you — specialties like the University of California at Berkeley's master's and doctoral programs in human ecology and environmental studies, appropriate for candidates concerned about urban blight, the harsh effects of urban development, or about the homeless; Yale School of Management for those interested in nonprofit management of schools, foundations, research organizations, and so on (the degree is an MPPM — master's in public and private management), although it is undergoing a restructuring of its program and emphases; Boston University's master's in arts management, which seeks candidates who will be running theaters, promoting rock concerts, acting as agents for entertainers or artists. The fewer the people in a specialty, the better your chances in many cases if you note that that specialty interests you (in some cases, however, the specialty is on the decline and more students are not sought). Aiming for that special niche where the competition is less intense is a sound strategy for many candidates who recognize that their credentials make them look-alikes with the competition.

You may turn up a specialty by talking to faculty. A professor may say to a prospective candidate for a master's in English literature: "Not much has been done here on Swift's poetry. Would you be interested in doing a thesis on it?" Of course this might not interest you, but your interest in the translation of Camus's novels might be similarly attractive to a different school.

When you have discovered one or more specialty slices in each of the programs to which you intend to apply, you can gather what your admissions prospects are. And this is where self-marketing comes in: when dealing with each admissions committee, enlarge on your own particular interest and competence in these specialties. Let's assume that the environment is your specialty and that you worked to eliminate chemical waste dumping in your community. You first find, through pie charts, those graduate programs that might have room for such a specialist, and then you market yourself as someone who will bring a special concern or flavor to a graduate program.

HOW PIE CHARTS HELP

Making pie charts for several graduate schools will help you see just where your chances of admission appear to be best. In Brad's case his chances at Columbia were improved by the nature of his employment. But what was true for Columbia did not appear to be so for MIT, because the average competitor there was so much stronger academically than Brad. He knew that his chances at MIT were marginal, and he was indeed turned down there.

If you are a woman, a member of a minority group, or a foreign applicant, your chances of admission may be better than those of other candidates to the same school, but you must be sensible about where you apply. It is not advisable to apply for admission to a program for which you are clearly not qualified. Being a woman from Alaska may give you an edge at eastern schools where the stiffest competition is among eastern candidates, but you must be capable of meeting the particular academic standards of the institution. As noted before, there are no free passes handed out to women, minorities, or foreigners applying to the highly selective graduate schools.

What about reverse discrimination, favoring minorities at the expense of more qualified nonminority applicants? In the famous Bakke case, the University of California's rejection of a white medical school applicant, Alan Bakke, was challenged on the grounds that his qualifications exceeded those of black applicants admitted. The U.S. Supreme Court ruled in 1978 that Bakke must be admitted and that no quotas could be established to assure a specific number of minority admissions.

At the same time the Court affirmed the institution's right to consider race, religion, ethnicity, and a history of a lack of academic opportunity as factors in admitting applicants. The result has been that some graduate programs pursue minority enrollment goals more vigorously than others. Minority applicants ought to acquaint themselves with the records of each program to which they apply. Some will obviously be more encouraging than others.

FIND YOUR COMBINATION OF SLICES

The more specialty slices of a pie chart that you can find yourself in, the better your chance of admission to that particular school. Take the two charts below as examples.

UNIVERSITY OF CHICAGO LAW SCHOOL ENTERING CLASS, 1988–89

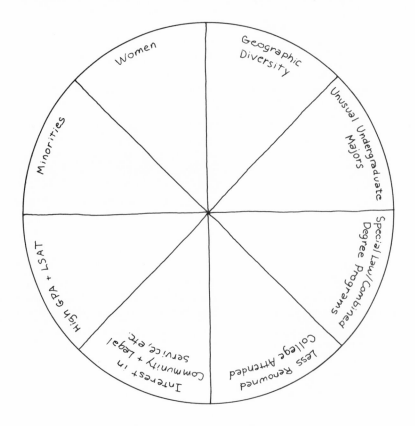

Profile of the class — Total enrollment: 174 (picked from 3,500 applicants)

Male	112	Average LSAT	44
Female	62	States represented	39
Minority students	13	Countries represented	13
International students	25	Undergraduate institutions	173
Average GPA	3.75		

continued

continued from page 136

*Geographic representation:

Northeast	187	Southwest	29
Southeast	45	Plains	31
Midwest	212	Far West	48

*These numbers total more than 174 because they include *all* law/combined degree enrollment.

THE WHARTON SCHOOL OF THE UNIVERSITY OF PENNSYLVANIA —
MBA PROGRAM ENTERING CLASS, 1987–88

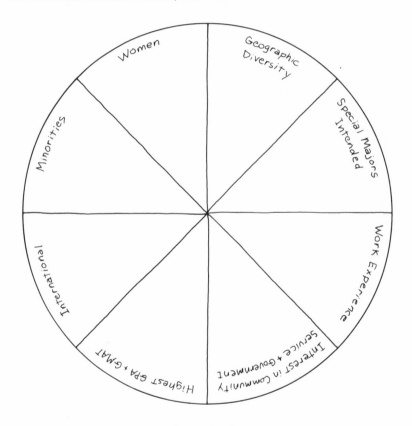

Profile of the class — Total enrollment: 750

continued

continued from page 137

Male 72%	Undergraduate majors:
Female 28%	Engineering 24%
Average age 26.5	Humanities and social
Minority students 16%	sciences 22%
International students.........17%	Business administration 21%
Full-time work experience......98%	Economics 20%
Average years of work	Science and
experience 3.9	mathematics.............. 9%
Average GPA 3.35	
Average GMAT 647	
States represented............ 44	
Countries represented 30	
Undergraduate institutions 123	

160 attended Ivy League institutions;
  20 came from Stanford alone.

Geographic representation:	Intended majors:
Northeast 28%	Management (including
Middle Atlantic 21%	entrepreneurial and
West 18%	multinational studies 31%
Living abroad 13%	Finance 27%
Midwest...............10%	Marketing.............16%
South.................10%	Transportation........... 3%
Notably, only a handful of students	Other.................23%
came from Texas.	

What these Wharton statistics indicate:

1. Northeastern candidates, especially those from the most competitive colleges, will have the most difficult admissions. GPA, GMAT, and general application quality must be at the top end of Wharton's profile.
2. Racial minority candidates from any section of the U.S. will have an excellent chance of admission if their GPA, GMAT, and quality of course background is solid. (Note that international students are not normally figured in as minority candidates.)
3. Women with *strong credentials* have a good chance of admission because the school's goal is to increase their representation well beyond the present 28 percent.
4. Applicants from the South and Midwest are in the smallest geo-

continued

continued from page 138

graphic pool and thus will stand a good chance of admission if their GPA and GMATs are strong.

5. The top-of-the-class student from a good but less-renowned college or state university may offer special appeal.
6. A senior in college will have virtually no chance of admission. Three to four years' work experience is a must. Other graduate programs will be a better bet, where 20 to 30 percent are accepted directly from college.
7. Interest in special programs that Wharton sponsors may stand out. Examples: the Lauder Institute for International Studies and Management; the combined Masters and MBA program offered in conjunction with Johns Hopkins School for Advanced International Studies; less popular MBA majors like manufacturing or transportation.
8. Well qualified international students are encouraged to apply and are accepted in good numbers.
9. Highly advanced or responsible level of work experience will help greatly.
10. Unusual work experience of an entrepreneurial, social service, or governmental nature will be attractive.

As you complete your pie charts, bear in mind that they are not just pointing you in the direction of graduate programs that will most likely admit you, but that they, again, provide you with a very sharp tool for marketing yourself. One student we counseled remarked that her pie chart revealed that she probably was the only applicant to several business schools who had traveled with Turkish relatives buying vegetable-dyed rugs from Anatolian peasants for resale in New York. In a personal statement on each application she told how her observation of the rug-making process helped her as an apprentice saleswoman sell these products.

WHAT MAKES YOU DIFFERENT?

In marketing yourself to any graduate program, it is also important to focus on one or two of your leading achievements or characteristics. Given the limited amount of time any committee member is going to be able to devote to a consideration of your application, you are doing him or her a service when you force attention only to one or two things that make you different — say, competence in a foreign language plus experience abroad in museum work if you are applying for admission to a graduate program in art history.

You target these valuable qualities in your essay and in your interview; you ask those who are recommending you to stress them if they will. One woman told us that she wrote all of her correspondence with graduate anthropology programs on the stationery of a Mexican farm cooperative where she was working as a volunteer; she wanted to make committees particularly aware of her qualifications to do field work under harsh conditions.

Here are some examples of how you can identify your strengths and target them for graduate admissions committees:

- A champion tennis player applying to medical schools constantly played up his athletic ability in order to demonstrate his manual skill, his stamina, his competitiveness. He even mentioned turning down an offer to go on the pro circuit because of his determination to go to medical school.
- A southerner with a modest academic and LSAT record, in applying to several prestigious northern law schools, made a big point of his lineage, which included a United States senator, two governors, a state supreme court justice, as well as some minor government officials and a law professor. His point was that he was driven by family tradition to make a name for himself. He was not saying that he could inherit success, but simply that a tradition of it gave him reason to work hard. He was admitted to a top law school.
- A woman who had been a national squash champion in college fixed admissions committees' attention on her social experience as an athlete, which she expected to turn into an asset as some kind of business manager. She was accepted into a Wharton MBA program and now has her own sports agency for women athletes.
- An anthropologist seeking the right Ph.D. program, after getting her masters at Columbia, wanted to be admitted to Cornell. Being a good pianist, she hit on the idea of using her talent to investigate native use of music for therapeutic purposes, and made the idea part of her successful application.
- A middle-aged journalist who had squeaked through college was admitted to a master's program in history at Columbia on the basis of articles he had written on the history of his New England hometown. He took the trouble to photocopy and package the articles in loose-leaf binders for easy reading and submitted them to four graduate schools, all of which admitted him.

In each of these cases the applicant marketed a strength in such a way that he or she stood out sufficiently to warrant admission. Thus they triumphed over others just as smart, just as accomplished, but less imaginative in their presentation of their strengths.

WHERE THE COMPETITION IS — AND ISN'T

This bar chart clearly shows that if you are applying to Wharton from the Northeast, you face considerably more competition for admission than anyone applying from other parts of the country. Of course you can't change your residence just to improve admission chances, but you can take note of where you live and determine whether or not your locality gives you an edge at a particular school. If it does not, then you should look to other qualities or criteria that make you exceptional enough to beat the competition; these can range from outstanding academic statistics to exceptional work experience.

BREAKDOWN OF SEPTEMBER MATRICULANTS IN WHARTON'S
MBA PROGRAM, BY ADDRESS OF APPLICATION

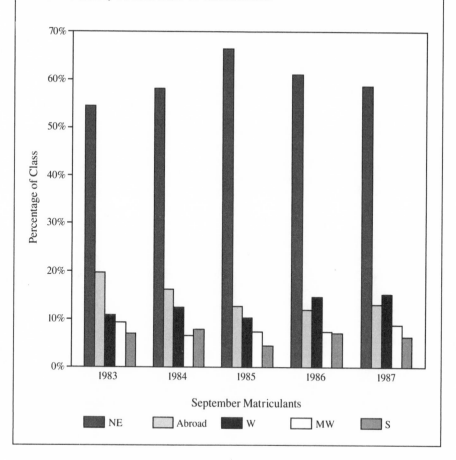

IDENTIFYING YOUR PARTICULAR STRENGTHS

There are some strengths that you may be proud of that admissions committees take for granted — your energy, your honesty, your forthrightness, sense of justice, marital stability, good health, and so on. You must always keep in mind that there are many, many applicants with such qualities. In regard to most of the qualities mentioned above, no graduate program would want anyone without them. What educators are looking for is evidence of capacity for strong graduate work. Experience shows that a person who has been capable of performing well at something honorable and constructive will probably do well in a graduate program, providing he or she has basic academic qualifications.

Admissions choices at the top and bottom are simple: the obviously brilliant are admitted and the obviously unqualified are rejected without discussion — these being the C students. It's the applicants in the middle who always trouble the members of graduate admissions committees — members of the faculty who will actually be teaching some if not all of those they admit.

"I hate to say it," says one such person, who prefers anonymity for obvious reasons, "but many of our decisions are purely arbitrary. We can take only so many applicants. Here is a group that by objective standards could be admitted and would complete the program satisfactorily. It then becomes a lottery as to who among these equals will be admitted." The candidate, then, who looks average but who has a specialty may be the candidate who is admitted, because he or she has managed to present something in his or her record that, as they say, jumps off the page.

How do you, if you are not an A student with high test scores, identify other strengths that will impress a graduate admissions committee? Well, let's go through the possibilities, including some already mentioned in previous chapters:

1. Exceptional extracurricular accomplishments — in college or thereafter. Among these are: athletic achievement; campus awards and nonscholastic honors; competitive achievement in such things as bridge, chess, public speaking; amateur theatrics (actors make good trial lawyers); writing for publications; managing athletic teams (some admissions committees are staffed with former athletes).
2. Work experience: This can be made meaningful by describing what you personally have learned on the job, even though the job may not have been part of a training program or an internship for the field you wish to study in. You must see your work as something unique to you, even when it may be routine. What you did to earn money for college may reveal a special talent.
3. Volunteer work and community activism: This can reveal a talent for organization, for getting along with people. One woman played up a single episode to schools of social work, a day when she helped handicapped skiers in a race in the White Mountains and found her life's

work to be in helping others. She was admitted to several strong programs.

4. Travel: In and of itself travel is commonplace and will not make you stand out. But if you have traveled to some unusual place like Yemen, well, at least this is out of the ordinary, and if you can make something of that experience other than a mere travelogue, if it has changed you in some significant way that bears on your desire for further education, a committee may take a closer look at your application — and that is the object of the exercise we call marketing your strengths. Yemen is mentioned because one candidate told political science admissions committees of being forced to turn over her car to Yemen bandits brandishing machine guns. It made her, she said, determine to specialize in the study of outlaws in the Middle East.

5. Marriage and child raising: Like travel, such experience usually signifies nothing very startling — in fact, committees may wonder if you can handle graduate work and a family as well. But what you have learned from marriage and raising children may be unusual enough to point out. A woman in her late thirties, who studied medicine at Harvard, said that she thinks they accepted her because she told the admissions committee that her experience with her own children made her want to be a pediatrician.

ADMISSIONS STRENGTHS ASSESSMENT

It may be helpful to work from a checklist in establishing those strengths that you can point to in self-marketing. (We are aware that we are repeating ourselves, but we also know from experience how frequently candidates fail to recognize their own strengths and hence do not do an adequate job of selling themselves to graduate admissions committees.)

- Academic strengths: While your grade point average and test scores tell most of the academic story, there may be something that does not appear in the record: a paper, an award, encouragement by a professor, a special project.
- Athletic and extracurricular strengths: This includes managing teams, and leadership activities. Continued athletic competition after graduation is often impressive as evidence of your physical fitness and energy. Mere membership in college organizations is not a strength. You must demonstrate some way you stand out, as an editor, chairman, president, lead actor, et cetera. Otherwise silence is advisable.

continued

continued from page 143
- Community involvement: Again, this must be significant to appear as a strength. Giving blood is not significant. Running a blood bank is. In the case of church activities, being in the choir will only appear to be a strength if you are applying for a music degree or possibly a divinity degree. But heading up the young people's group or being in charge of a food-distribution program is a strength.
- Work experience: Particularly for MBA applicants, work experience can be crucial. Your interpretation of the value of a job and its relationship to a graduate program will determine its usefulness as an admissions factor.
- Other strengths: This can be any strength peculiar to you. If you are handicapped and have learned how to be effective within your limitations, this is an enormous strength. Or you may have overcome personal problems in order to complete your education. You may be proud of your family background and its tradition of service.

HOW TO MARKET YOUR STRENGTHS

Assuming that you have identified the graduate programs you think you are qualified for, and that you have determined the strengths that you would like to call attention to, you have, as noted earlier, the following opportunities to market yourself:

- your application as a whole
- personal statements in particular
- interviews
- recommendations
- meetings with faculty

Let us go back to Brad Huntley and follow his steps as a candidate.

Here are the self-marketing aspects of his application:

Among other things, Brad had this to say in his personal statement:

"I believe my mediocre academic performance in college was due to lack of motivation. I was already making money in real estate and could not relate my coursework to business. Then, as my experience in selling commercial property broadened, I found myself doing business with men and women who frequently challenged my assertions. After a few deals fell through, I learned from a competitor (no friend) that I was considered too cocky and not believable. I was getting by in many cases on fast talk.

"That's when I began reading something more than trade magazines. Because I was continually contacting various municipal boards about variances, land use, and such things, I took a night course in municipal government at SUNY Albany and got an A. I know that I would have no trouble in doing MBA level work. . . .

"I really feel that my experience in regional real estate is unusual for someone my age. I consider myself a pro now, but a pro limited to a niche that offers only limited opportunities. The course content of Columbia's new MBA program looks to me like a pathway to really major real estate dealings. I want the chance to move into an urban realty operation (not necessarily in New York City). But at present my ambitions are greater than my qualifications. An MBA, I think, can move me into a bigger arena."

In his interview Brad continually referred to his experience as a top salesman of commercial real estate.

For references Brad used two undergraduate professors and two professionals in real estate, telling them that he was emphasizing his practical success, since his academic record and test scores spoke for themselves, and suggesting that they relate their comments to his work. Of course the college professors could only say in passing that they understood he had made good use of his undergraduate training in his work in real estate, but this was one more pinch of salt.

ONE MAN'S STRENGTHS

We have so far talked only in general terms about Brad's ability to sell commercial real estate. Actually he defined his strengths in very specific terms, as follows:

"I am a detail man. I have to know everything about a property before I begin to market it.

"I never exaggerate nor do I conceal anything I know from a potential buyer.

"I always investigate a potential buyer's qualifications, financial and professional. I have on occasion broken off a negotiation after discovering something unfavorable about a buyer.

"I have studied government regulations concerning land use, and made myself knowledgeable about perc testing, building codes, bank practices, tenant habits, and so on."

In other words, Brad presented himself as someone who was already a student of real estate in his area, and who wanted to expand in terms of his knowledge into a larger world.

Some people fantasize about their strengths and present their aspirations instead of their accomplishments. In contrast, Brad knew his strengths and how they applied to his educational aspirations and expressed this.

MARKETING YOUR PASSION

Sandra Anton's passion as an undergraduate at Harvard was neglected children. She worked in a city program teaching fifth- and sixth-graders dance and theater, and she was so appalled when state funds for it were eliminated that she became an intern in a public-service law firm specializing in cases representing the rights of children. Here is part of her personal statement in applying to law schools:

"More than once I have been called a 'woman of the '80s.' If this means that I have seized every available opportunity, then I suppose the proverbial shoe fits. I've been co-founder and owner of my own business, a quarterly publication for Boston-area college and graduate students, and served as both business editor and special publications manager of the Harvard daily newspaper.

"While taking advantage of all that college has had to offer, I have continued to participate in programs centered around children, my primary field of interest. The stark contrast between the world of opportunity available to me and the universe of obstacles faced by children of low-income families has proven impossible for me to ignore. One response on my part has been to adopt a 'little sister' named Keri, who lives in a Cambridge housing project with her unwed mother.

"One way I helped Keri was to introduce her to City Step, a community dance-theater activity. . . . But on returning to college in September I was outraged to discover that legislative budget cuts eliminated this program in the public schools.

"My new project was to intern at Lawyers for Children, an organization whose work includes helping foster children. I was able to help one child, Chris, who was for some time a bureaucratic victim, unable to return to his own home where he was truly wanted. This experience revealed to me how flawed the juvenile court system is. I am now seeking a legal education in the hopes of serving children like Keri and Chris. I hope to prove that I am no mere 'woman of the '80s,' but a woman with a heart and mind and goals for many future decades."

A FAMILY BUSINESS CAN BE A STRENGTH

Do you expect to enter a family business? Some applicants might consider this to be reliance on nepotism rather than a strength, but MBA programs like students who are assured of a future in a successful business. You must stress, however, that you do not wish to advance simply through connections, but through expertise. One MBA applicant wrote the following:

"My family has been manufacturing shoes in Maine for almost a century. Without hesitation I have always accepted my father's wish that I join his firm after completing my education at Bates College. Now, after three years' work in every department of the company, I am assistant sales manager, and while I am pleased with my work I am uneasy about the future in this highly competitive business which has been so impacted by foreign competition.

"My father agrees with my idea of seeking an MBA to prepare me for a changing economic environment. Our business needs new machinery. A consultant has been hired to advise us on the best way to raise capital. I want to be able to make the right kind of decisions for our company as I advance up the ladder. Tradition is not enough to sustain a successful company today. We are going to have to develop innovative marketing techniques, and it is hard to credit but we are looking into opening an offshore manufacturing unit.

"I would hope that an MBA would be enormously helpful to me in the next few years. Someday I hope I will have earned the right to be our company's CEO — through hard work, but also through an understanding of how to meet new and unexpected management problems. I very much want to spend two years learning how others have met business challenges."

SELF-MARKETING FOR LIBERAL ARTS AND SCIENCE GRADUATE PROGRAMS

When it comes to admittance to a nonprofessional program in the liberal arts or sciences, the self-marketing of the applicant should begin in college. Almost everything depends on one or more faculty recommendations so far as distinguished graduate programs in the top universities are concerned. An outstanding student will have no problem getting into some kind of a graduate program, but if you have your eye on Wisconsin, Stanford, Johns Hopkins, Princeton, or others in this category of excellence, your GPA and test scores alone may not be enough. The great research universities are looking for students who have been observed by their undergraduate professors to be remarkable.

Since scholarly students often are shy and not overly social, they may fail to impress their teachers despite their papers and examination records. Such students get good recommendations to good graduate schools, but not always to the best, for such recommendations are few, reserved for the most promising. It is therefore up to you to make your qualities known to key faculty. How do you do this without appearing obsequious?

You first of all make your objectives known. Good teachers like to train good teachers or good researchers. A student who from the start talks of plans to do scholarly work in English literature at Yale will quickly find out if this ambition is reasonable. Either a teacher will point out what must be done to become eligible for such graduate work, or a teacher will begin to pay more attention to such a student, ask for more work, suggest possible lines of research, help get a paper published, arrange for some summer study program. (In the case of a scientific field, the teacher might additionally set up an experiment to be worked on.)

You must pick your favorite faculty member, if you are not first of all picked by someone, with an eye to the record: What has happened to his or her former students? The faculty member you feel most comfortable with may be less of a scholar than his or her colleagues. And the great star may not have time for you, being off in Washington a lot, or consulting off-campus.

A virtue of early self-marketing is that you may very well be directed toward a particularly good program that a faculty member is intimate with. Your undergraduate work can then be shaped to meet a specific need. If you learn early on of a new Latin American art history program at NYU and are interested in it, you can cover ground in undergraduate work that will be helpful to you later.

SELF-MARKETING CAN ONLY HELP

Suppose you are Phi Beta Kappa, even a Rhodes Scholar with an Oxford degree: Are you right to assume that self-marketing is beneath you? We rather doubt it. The fact is that graduate schools like to be sold on candidates. They do not resist marketing efforts at all, for from them they learn more about the candidates. It is a mistake to think that graduate schools are cold and impersonal, riveted by a numbers watch, indifferent to the individual character they are considering.

It is therefore very important to take Step Eight seriously, however qualified you are. There are in most cases many others like you, and there are only so many places in each graduate class. To make sure that you occupy one, market yourself.

Step Eight Checklist

1. Work out a self-marketing program as part of your attempt to qualify for graduate work. It is an essential element in the competition for admission to the better programs.

2. Try to avoid false modesty or exaggeration.

3. Make use of class profiles and pie charts to find small slices you fit into, in order to help you market yourself to programs to which you have the best chances of being admitted.

4. Identify your strengths and call attention to them when appropriate in the admissions process.

5. Even if you are a top candidate, market yourself. Admissions committees welcome the candidate who puts his or her best foot forward.

STEP NINE

Examine the Many Ways to Finance Graduate Work

GRADUATE SCHOOL IS COSTLY BUT FEASIBLE

We do not wish to play Pollyanna when we say that the high cost of graduate education should not be allowed to stand in the way of earning a postgraduate degree. But despite the heavy monetary burden, thousands of strapped graduate students continue their studies successfully. However, for some, financing their education is less nerve-racking than it is for others. The difference lies in their willingness to take the time and make the effort to plan ahead, and to take advantage of the many opportunities they discover in their search for sources of funds.

You no doubt are aware that graduate school: (a) costs more than undergraduate education; (b) often imposes a heavy debt burden; (c) may necessitate the postponement, for a year or more, of studies in order to accumulate required money; (d) has limited available government aid; (e) usually makes working your way through unadvisable, because the heavy academic load allows so little time for a part-time job, and because it is important that you do well in grad school where less than a B-minus grade is a failure.

Our theme then is: We never promised you a rose garden. Graduate school means hard work academically, and financing its costs means making sacrifices for all but the well-to-do. But because you are intelligent and energetic enough to do graduate work, you can meet this financing challenge with the same determination and drive that will land you in a graduate program.

THE RANGE OF GRADUATE TUITION COSTS

Here is the average cost of annual tuition at various graduate schools:

Private Institutions

Public Institutions

Medical school $14,750

Medical school $6,500 (resident); $12,500 (out of state)

Law school $13,675

Law school $3,260 (resident); $6,710 (out of state)

Business school $13,500

Business school $3,300 (resident); $6,150 (out of state)

Engineering/science $13,400

Engineering/science $1,790 (resident); $4,675 (out of state)

Liberal arts, master's $12,015

Liberal arts, master's $4,514 (resident); $9,446 (out of state)

Note: The number of years usually required to earn the graduate degree is:

M.D.	4
LL.B	3
MBA	2
M.A. or M.S.	1 to 2
Ph.D.	2 to 3 years of coursework. A research thesis can take two to five additional years, during which tuition is not charged.

ANOTHER FINANCIAL AID SYSTEM

If you received financial aid in college, you will recall how you went about securing what was called a financial aid package that consisted of a grant or scholarship, a loan, and a part-time job of about fifteen hours a week. What you did was to file with the College Scholarship Service a needs analysis Financial Aid Form (FAF) in collaboration with your parents, whose income and general financial situation (home ownership, number of children in college, et cetera) determined the amount of the aid package. This determination is based on an elaborate formula that includes federal criteria set by the U.S. Department of Education.

Some graduate programs also use the FAF, but a far larger number ask applicants to file a financial statement on a GAPSFAS form, used by over 100,000 applicants and 700 institutions. GAPSFAS stands for Graduate and Professional School Financial Aid Service, which, like the College Scholarship Service, is run by the Educational Testing Service in Princeton, New Jersey. It is a centralized application and needs analysis service. From information furnished by the applicant, GAPSFAS submits a needs analysis to the graduate school, which then makes its own determination as to the amount of aid it can offer an applicant.

GAPSFAS does not control the size or character of aid to be distributed. It simplifies data and suggests appropriate aid; the institutions, however, make their own decisions according to their resources and to the intensity of their interest in the applicant (if they want someone badly, they may offer a bigger aid package than GAPSFAS suggests).

THE SOAR REPORT

The GAPSFAS analysis of your filed financial statement is known by the ironic acronym SOAR (Summary of Applicant's Resources), suggestive of the rising costs of graduate education. The SOAR report analyzes the applicant's resources, including any parental contribution that the applicant says will be made, the applicant's savings, available academic year income, and available assets of the applicant and/or spouse. If the applicant is a dependent of his or her parents, GAPSFAS also examines the parents' means in order to determine what they can reasonably loan or contribute toward graduate education, according to GAPSFAS criteria based on national norms and bearing in mind that parents are not expected to make as large a sacrifice as they did for the same applicant's undergraduate costs. If the applicant is supporting children, an allowance for this expense is factored in.

The formula for deriving the suggested aid to be arranged by the institution is complex and of relatively passing interest to the applicant, since once the financial statement is filed, it goes into a computer, where the program automatically determines suggested aid figures.

We reiterate that it is important to be aware of a graduate school's option to use the SOAR report according to its own available resources. In general, the richer the institution, the more aid an applicant can expect. But institutions with limited funds may nonetheless selectively distribute them with considerable largess in order to attract applicants they want in their programs. In this sense, there is a merit basis to aid, particularly to that distributed by the great research universities, but even to aid from the so-called second-tier institutions.

So, if you think you can compete against the better applicants for admission to the more competitive programs, you should do so because of the educational advantages such programs offer, and because of the more alluring future that can be anticipated. At the same time you should not neglect to apply to the second-tier programs, because they may offer you more aid. You will then have to decide whether to sacrifice more aid in order to be in a more prestigious program.

HOW GRADUATE FINANCES DIFFER FROM UNDERGRADUATE

Why is it more difficult to finance graduate education than undergraduate education?

1. Graduate education is more expensive for the schools because it is labor intensive — no large lecture courses. Graduate students work closely with faculty, whose salaries are higher than those of undergraduate faculty.
2. Graduate schools lack the extensive endowed scholarship programs and thus cannot always make a commitment to aid all who qualify for admission.
3. Only the top research institutions have the funds to finance all the students they want in their graduate programs.
4. Graduate students frequently arrive with an undergraduate debt burden.
5. Part-time work is less feasible for graduate students because of the heavy academic burden imposed by graduate programs.

On the positive side, the difficulty of financing graduate education has been recognized by the federal government and by state governments too. Their programs currently offer more promise of financial relief to graduate students than to undergraduates. Also, the attractiveness of state university graduate programs is enormous because, as we have seen, tuition can be less than half that of private programs. Finally, military programs sometimes provide tuition relief to graduate students who have formerly been with the service.

RANGE OF LIVING-EXPENSE BUDGETS

One of the guidelines that determines what financial aid a graduate school applicant may receive is the range of basic nine-month living expenses, including housing, food, and clothing budgets, set by the Bureau of Labor Statistics, as follows:

Student's Marital Status	Nine Months' Expenses	
	BLS Lower Standard	*BLS Intermediate Standard*
Single	$ 4,059	$ 6,714
Married — no children	6,054	9,014
Married — 1 child	7,986	11,893
Married — 2 children	9,532	14,195
Married — 3 children	12,108	18,031

THE MANY WAYS TO FINANCE GRADUATE EDUCATION

Over the years private and public agencies have worked together to ease the graduate student's financial burdens (before World War II there was hardly any money at all available to aid graduate students). To take advantage of this, you should begin as early as possible to work out two figures: (1) what your graduate education will probably cost, and (2) what you can reasonably expect in aid from all sources.

There are three basic categories of money available for a graduate student's education: (1) grants, fellowships, and scholarships — outright contributions from government programs (including GI Bill assistance), educational institutions, foundations, corporations, and other private sources; (2) education-related salaries, such as those paid for teaching assistantships, research assistantships, administrative internships or assistantships, dormitory and counseling assistantships, college work-study programs, or, secondarily, salaries for jobs in the community, unrelated to the graduate school; (3) loans from government, institutional, or private sources.

When a graduate program offers a student an aid package, it includes some combination of the three categories above — outright contributions, loans on which interest must be paid and which must eventually be repaid, and jobs at its disposal, usually within the graduate institution. Thus the word "aid" has three meanings: free funds that are a gift, funds that must be repaid with interest, and funds for which services are performed.

In addition we should mention the possibility of an employer's financing graduate education and, again, the opportunities for graduate work at federal expense if you are a member of the armed services or of certain government bureaus or agencies, like the State Department. Some aid is available only to minority and women applicants.

GAPSFAS — A VERY PERSONAL FINANCIAL STATEMENT

Only after you have determined the bottom line, i.e., the aid you will need to fill the gap between your resources and the estimated cost of your graduate education, should you file a GAPSFAS statement. The GAPSFAS financial statement is a four-page form with about seventy-nine items to fill in. Its object is to determine the financial status of the applicant, his or her spouse, and his or her parents, in order to be able to determine fairly how much aid he or she deserves. It is straightforward, but searching to the point that it may try your patience. For example, you will probably need one or more of the following records:

- U.S. and state income tax returns for yourself and family
- W-2 forms and other records of money earned last year

- Records of untaxed income — social security, welfare, veterans benefits, et cetera
- Current bank statements
- Current mortgage information
- Records of last year's medical and dental bills
- Business and farm records
- Investment records

Well, most graduate school applicants seeking aid should not have anything to hide. But suppose an applicant is considered a dependent of his or her parents and will receive some support while in graduate school. In that case the parents are asked to disclose their financial position on the application for graduate school aid. As we told our readers in *Scaling the Ivy Wall,* there really is no reason parents should disclose to their children details of their personal finances. Therefore, we suggest that the applicant fill in his or her sections, then turn the GAPSFAS form over to the parents for completion and mailing.

ARE YOU A DEPENDENT OF YOUR PARENTS?

You are considered a dependent of your parents if:

1. you live with them more than six weeks of the year;
2. your parents claim you as an income tax exemption; and
3. you receive more than $750 in support from them.

GAPSFAS MAY BE ONLY THE BEGINNING

If your graduate school aid package leaves you short, and it often does, then you must seek out other sources of aid yourself — in the form of scholarships, fellowships, grants, and loans (which are often distributed outside of a particular graduate school's auspices), corporate aid, or personal savings.

After filing a GAPSFAS report, applicants to professional schools — law, medicine, business, engineering, et cetera — usually obtain most of their aid through the school in which they enroll. Graduate students in the humanities and sciences are more likely to be awarded specific fellowships for which they must make separate application in addition to their GAPSFAS report.

BIG ENDOWMENTS MEAN MORE AVAILABLE
FINANCIAL AID

Institutions with significant endowments are anxious to enroll top students, often in small programs. In the following form letter Vanderbilt sends to applicants to its Owen Graduate School of Management the phrase "concentrate our resources on academic excellence" means not only spending money for top faculty but that the university also has ample scholarship funds to attract the ablest students.

Owen Graduate School of Management

VANDERBILT UNIVERSITY

 NASHVILLE, TENNESSEE 37203   TELEPHONE (615) 322-2534

Office of Admission and Student Services • Direct phone 322-6469

Dear Prospective MBA Student:

Thank you for inquiring about the Vanderbilt MBA program. Enclosed you will find information about admission, scholarships and financial aid, and the Owen School in general.

Included are:

1. Application for Admission; Letter of Recommendation forms and a Transcript Request form.
2. *A Prospectus.*
3. "Scholarship and Financial Aid, 1987-88."
4. MBA Scholarship Application.
5. Graduate Management Admission Test order form.
6. "Candidate's Admission Calendar."
7. "The Honor System."
8. Campus Map.

With an enrollment of just 300 regular MBA students, the Owen School is one of the smallest of the 16 schools in the United States that are devoted exclusively to MBA education. Our relatively small enrollment has enabled us to concentrate our resources on academic excellence, and, at the same time, to accentuate a personal approach to graduate management education.

I am pleased to share this information about the Owen School with you and look forward to hearing from you with any questions you may have after you have reviewed it.

Sincerely yours,

Joel B. Covington, Jr.
Acting Director

encls.

JBC/jw

continued from page 156

The financial aid brochure mentioned describes available aid as:

- ten full-tuition and twenty half-tuition scholarships, awarded annually to top students;
- Owen grants of $2,000 to $5,000 based on need, to be applied against tuition of $12,000;
- four kinds of student loans;
- college work-study jobs.

FINDING GRANTS AND FELLOWSHIPS

Grants and fellowships may fall in your lap, but usually you have to make an effort to find and apply for them. They are the cream of financial aid, being outright gifts to meet the cost of graduate study. The distinction between a grant and a fellowship is that a grant is awarded for need and a fellowship for merit. The brilliant scholar can be a millionaire and still seek a fellowship, not because of greed but for the prestige of the award. The term "scholarship" usually applies to undergraduate awards, but is sometimes used to mean either a graduate grant or fellowship.

The sources of grants and fellowships are: states, corporations, foundations, and the U.S. Department of Education. You will be able to get some more specific guidance in your search from the graduate programs to which you apply, but probably not much. You will in all likelihood be directed to a shelf of materials related to grants and fellowships, and you can work from them to other sources in libraries. You will need to make phone calls and write letters as you seek to discover what monies you can conceivably apply for.

An initial discovery may be a description like the one of the Fannie and John Hertz Foundation Graduate Fellowship Program, which appears on pages 158–159. The following bibliography may prove useful as you start your search:

A Guide to Scholarships, Fellowships, and Grants: A Selected Bibliography, Kathleen Slowik and Diane D'Angelo. Institute of International Education, 809 United Nations Plaza, New York, NY 10017.

Free Money for Professional Studies, Laurie Blum. New York: Barnes and Noble Books, Harper and Row, 1985.

Grants for Graduate Students, 1986–88. Andrea Leskes, editor. Peterson's Guides, Box 2123, Princeton, NJ 08543-2123.

The Individual's Guide to Grants, Judith B. Margolin. New York: Plenum Press, 1983.

HARVARD'S GUIDE TO GRANTS

Every year Harvard publishes *The Graduate Guide to Grants,* a 200-page listing of aid programs — from those offered by the American Council of the Blind to those offered by the State Historical Society of Wisconsin. Just a glance at the table of contents shows a variety of funding for special scholarly interests such as Turkish studies, visual arts, Islamic architecture, foreign currency, Jewish culture, microbiology, and environmental conservation. How to tap into this cornucopia of financial aid?

Cynthia Verba, Director of Fellowships and author of this guide, lists no less than thirteen steps in her suggestions as to how to use this information. "For the most effective use of this Guide," she writes, "it is important to bear in mind that the process of gathering information about existing fellowships is something like a research project itself."

Among ways to carry out such a project, she says, are:

• consulting fellowship files in libraries;
• consulting other sources, such as those we list in this book;
• consulting faculty for advice;
• consulting the *Foundation Grants Index* of 10,000 fellowships offered by over 300 foundations;
• consulting Educational Testing Service's *Graduate and Professional School Opportunities for Minority Students.*

Applying for a fellowship is a highly competitive process. The actual application must be crafted to meet the requirements of the individual fellowship. A persuasive description of the project or study the applicant will carry out will help win the fellowship.

HOW A $15,000 FELLOWSHIP IS DESCRIBED

Here is an entry from the grant summaries in Harvard's *Graduate Guide to Grants:*

Fannie and John Hertz Foundation
Graduate Fellowship Program
Post Office Box 2230
Livermore, CA 94550-0130
(415) 449-0855

continued

continued from page 158

CONTACT: Kathryn Smith, Assistant Secretary

PURPOSE: To promote education and enhancement of the defense potential and technological stature of the United States, by aiding in the education of the most capable students, particularly with respect to application of the physical sciences.

ELIGIBILITY: Applications are accepted from seniors as well as from students who have already commenced graduate study. The proposed field of study must be concerned with applications of physical sciences to human problems. No joint Ph.D./professional degree programs are supported. United States citizenship, or documented evidence of application to acquire it, is required of all applicants. The Foundation requires all Fellows to morally commit themselves to make their skills and abilities available for common defense, in the event of national emergency.

TENURE AND VALUE: The duration of the Fellowship is one academic year and applications can be made for a renewal. The full annual stipend is $15,000. The Foundation also pays an educational allowance up to $8,000 to the academic institution for the Fellow's proposed program of study. Fellowship funds are disbursed by the Fellow's school.

APPLICATION: Applications can be attained upon written or telephone request to the Foundation's office. The application deadline is November 1.

Close to 200 grants are listed in this annual publication, which can be obtained by writing to:
Office of Student Affairs
Byerly Hall
Cambridge, MA 02138

SUPPORT FOR UNDERGRADUATES CONTEMPLATING GRADUATE SCHOOL

Yale's University Career Services lists a number of sources of aid for which you may apply as an undergraduate, of which the following are specifically for those planning to go to graduate school:

* Collaborative Research Grants (Fulbright Program) — To fund proposals for joint research abroad by teams of two or three graduating seniors, graduate students, or postdoctoral researchers.

* Marshall Scholarships — For graduating seniors and others under twenty-six years of age with a B.A. to support two years of study at a university in the United Kingdom.

Other aid sources listed by Yale which are of possible relevance to future graduate students include Mellon Foundation Fellowships in the Humanities, National Science Foundation Graduate Fellowships, and Minority Graduate Fellowships.

Similar lists are compiled by most universities and colleges sending many graduates on to further education. Note that all these programs, grants, and scholarships are administered at the college or university, in this case Yale, but the programs are of course open to students throughout the country. In other words, you don't have to go to Yale to be a Marshall Scholar or earn a Mellon Foundation Fellowship.

COPING WITH LOANS

"Neither a borrower, nor a lender be," said Polonius, but this old saw must be ignored by most graduate students, for whom debt is a fact of life. A congressional report done in 1987 found that a third to a half of all students leave college with debts. Public college graduates on the average owe $6,685, and private college graduates, $8,950. While those who prepared the report were obviously uneasy about overburdening a debtor generation, the report of the Congressional Joint Economic Committee suspended judgment as to the dangers of this situation.

Of concern is the simultaneous decline in federal grants; borrowing is rising to replace this source of undergraduate aid. Federal loans rose more than fourfold in a decade from the mid-1970s to 1985–86, while federal grants and scholarships fell by one-third. Some 4.7 million college and graduate students borrowed from the federal government in 1985–86, three times the number who did ten years earlier.

It is contended by some that the rise in student borrowing is not a consequence of there being less federal grant money, but is a function of greatly increased college costs. In any case, the borrowing goes on, and the debt burden is hardest on students with the least means. But even the middle-class students feel the impact of money owed at graduation time. Educators are perplexed as to how to deal with this; there are modest moves being made in Congress to increase grants to graduate students.

Meanwhile, however, borrowing from the government, universities, and banks continues to rise. You, as a graduate student, must somehow manage your finances so as to avoid an indebtedness that forces you to make life decisions that are against your instincts.

Since you probably will need a loan, the graduate programs to which you apply for admission will usually include in their aid packages one or more loans from any of these federal loan sources — Guaranteed Student Loans, PLUS Loans, National Direct Student Loans, Health Education Assistance Loans, Health Professional Loans, and Sallie Mae's "GradEd Financing" program for professional students in a dozen states. All of these loans are administered through the financial aid offices of the graduate schools, so there is no need for an applicant to approach any federal government bureau directly. Any questions you have about these loans should be directed to the graduate schools.

Almost any graduate student can borrow money at 5 percent from the National Direct Student Loan Program, at 8 percent from the Guaranteed Student Loan Program, and at 12 percent from the PLUS Loan Program. Getting the money is no problem. It's paying the interest and eventually discharging the debt that makes smart people pause. Monthly payments on $10,000 at 8 percent come to about $121. If loan repayments are postponed until graduate study is finished, the Ph.D. candidate may be paying off debt while working on his or her dissertation as an unenrolled student.

Some graduate programs can also arrange for you to borrow directly from the college or university where you are doing graduate work. Independently of the college you can, if need be, arrange for a bank loan if your credit is good. There are home equity loans for families willing to take out second mortgages.

We are not financial consultants, so we must leave to each graduate student the individual decision about what is a reasonable debt burden. A doctor may start out owing $50,000 and so accept a salaried position in a health-care facility in order to be sure he or she will be able to liquidate the debt eventually. A liberal arts student may prefer to work a year or more as a waiter to build up savings rather than borrow. A family may sell a second home to help a child through graduate school.

Despite the congressional moves mentioned above, we think it fair to say that, unlike those in many countries, government agencies in the United States do not put a high priority on financing graduate education. Our graduate students are obliged to bird-dog it, tracking down money wherever the scent leads. We can only warn that one easy scent is loan money, and this track should be the last one you choose to follow, and the least made use of. Easier said than done.

DRAW YOUR OWN FINANCIAL PLAN

A graduate student financial plan requires no knowledge of high finance, just a knowledge of opportunities and limitations. Without a plan, your graduate studies may be interrupted by lack of funds, never to be resumed once you start working and perhaps raising a family.

What may relieve anxiety and help you to avoid such an interruption is a financial plan based on reality, and a willingness to anticipate the consequences of your debt burden. To say, "I'll pay off my debt by working for a law factory, much as I hate the idea," is not the most sound kind of financial planning. Better to postpone school a year or two, save some money, then get through law school and engage in the kind of practice you love.

The steps to take in preparing such a plan are easy enough to enumerate:

1. Estimate all costs of graduate education through the granting of a degree.
2. Examine the possibility of studying at your state university, where costs are considerably lower than at private institutions. In other words, don't conclude that a state program is necessarily inferior to a more prestigious private program. (You have only to think that Wisconsin residents in some University of Wisconsin graduate programs may be getting degrees equal to any in the country.)
3. Study the reasonable sacrifices you can make to meet graduate education costs.
4. Take months if need be to make an exhaustive search for aid programs that will help pay your way.
5. Ask these questions: Is there an employer who will help finance my degree (most pertinent for MBA applicants)? Will military service offer a free graduate education without too much lost career time? Am I going to have to put too much time in on jobs to enable me to do well in my academic work? Have I talked to the right faculty and administrative people about my financial needs? Am I asking my parents to help me, knowing that in time I can repay their kindness?
6. Contact administrators of fellowship programs for information on how to make a strong application; study a "how-to" book on grantsmanship such as *The Individual's Guide to Grants* by Judith B. Margolin (New York: Plenum Press, 1983).
7. Finally, list all possible sources of funds available to you and make sure they add up to the amount you need. This way, you will not be plagued with that insidious worry about money when your mind should be on your graduate work.

SAMPLE FINANCIAL WORKSHEET

Graduate Schools	1. _____	2. _____	3. _____
Costs			
Tuition	_____	_____	_____
Living expenses	_____	_____	_____
Fees	_____	_____	_____
Books and supplies	_____	_____	_____
Travel	_____	_____	_____
Other	_____	_____	_____
Total one-year budget	_____	_____	_____
Sources of Funds			
Savings	_____	_____	_____
Earnings, one year	_____	_____	_____
Parents' contribution	_____	_____	_____
Spouse's contribution	_____	_____	_____
Fellowships	_____	_____	_____
Federal and state aid administered by graduate school	_____	_____	_____
Loans	_____	_____	_____
Total available	_____	_____	_____

IT CAN BE DONE

Without underestimating the financial burden of many graduate programs, we wish to encourage anyone seeking a good graduate degree not to abandon such a wonderful project for purely financial reasons. It may be necessary to postpone graduate studies in order to save a sufficient sum for completing a program. It may be that you will have to stretch out the number of years of actual study as you work to support yourself. But we say from experience with many graduate students of modest means that financing graduate work can be done.

The fact is, it is being done, as the number of new graduate students rises in this country by 1.5 percent a year. Which is to say: If you don't get the degree you want, someone else will, whatever the financial obstacles.

We hope that you will follow this Step Nine and that it will help you to surmount difficulties in financing your further education. Don't miss the opportunity of a lifetime because you can't afford it. You can afford it if you really want it. What you can't afford is to disappoint yourself by not applying to a good program and applying for an aid package. What happens after that will depend on your ingenuity and determination. We are betting that you can do it!

Step Nine Checklist

1. Study very carefully the financial aid data of each institution you plan to apply to.
2. File the requisite forms for financial aid — GAPSFAS if required.
3. Research such other aid opportunities as grants, fellowships, and corporate backing.
4. When borrowing, make sure you will be able to afford interest payments and reduction of principal.
5. Explore alternate graduate programs in your field to see what the range of costs is.
6. Determine the maximum amount of money you can expect from your own and family resources. Make up a tentative financial plan.
7. Take time off to save money rather than stealing study time to pursue part-time jobs in graduate school.
8. When aid has been allotted by the graduate program you plan to enter, and you have all other support lined up, draw up a final financial plan.

Complete the Admissions Process Scrupulously

Having taken the first nine essential steps toward applying to a graduate program, you now must be careful not to stumble on the tenth step, which consists of actually completing a number of applications, some quite different from others; considering the possibility of interviews and visits to institutions; and, finally, choosing among programs that accept you. These activities are unusual. You are doing them for the first time. You may say that you went through this routine when you applied to college, but remember that was some years ago, and graduate school is not college. The wise applicant completes the admissions process with the greatest of care, because it is at the culminating point of a crucial personal presentation.

In the prior steps you have sought to construct a record of academic and nonacademic accomplishments that speaks for itself; you have sought to match your capabilities to some graduate programs you believe are right for you. Many others have done the same thing. Admissions committees will therefore be looking for further evidence of your qualifications, and they will be sensitive to signs of immaturity, particularly as seen in any carelessness in your application.

THE APPLICATION IS YOU

"Sad to say, but we reject a number of candidates every year simply because of sloppy applications," says Stephen Christakos of the Wharton School of Business at the University of Pennsylvania. "We have enough good candidates to choose from, and we think that anyone who won't take the time to prepare an application with scrupulous thoroughness will not do satisfactory graduate work."

It would be a shame to be denied admission to a fine graduate program just because you were too casual in completing your application.

An application form of any sort tends to look dry, lifeless, and forbidding in its cold requests for information or self-revelation. Initial reactions as applicants complete this crucial admissions document may range from boredom and indifference to outright hostility. Beware, though: A sloppy application at the very least shows that the candidate has not taken it as seriously as he or she should.

It seems so obvious that an application to any graduate program should be carefully drawn up; it should hardly be necessary to dwell on such things as the need to study application instructions, to read through each application before filling it in, to proofread your applications for typos, to check for spelling errors, to meet deadlines, to make sure your college transcript is sent in to the proper office, and to check that recommendations have been sent in by faculty, employers, or others. You must also be sure to sign each application and always enclose the fee.

Attention to detail is essential. We urge you to take the time to complete a perfect application, error free, easy to read, providing all the information required. You must remember that this is the chief document in your file, one that may be reviewed several times by different committee members. It is the equivalent of a self-portrait, a text that says: This is ME.

You should, therefore, we remind you again, study application forms early in the admissions process, because the graduate application is more complex than an undergraduate application. You are now a mature adult, for whom few if any allowances are made for error.

As an example of mistakes to be avoided, a number of careless applicants every year have their transcripts sent directly to one or more law schools instead of to the Law School Data Assembly service of the Law School Admission Council/Law School Admission Services in Newtown, Pennsylvania. This is not fatal, but it delays processing the application and can make a bad impression if an admissions committee member learns about it from a person in the office who had to return your transcript to you for resubmission.

A typical slip is to forget to include the application fee, without which the application sits unprocessed until your check arrives.

Some applicants neglect to sign their applications. Others ignore deadlines. Or they fail to tell those sending in letters of recommendation to write their names across the envelope seal, as some admissions committees request. Programs requesting that the application be typed receive applications in longhand. The possibilities of goofing are considerable.

To keep the application process orderly, you should maintain a few files:

1. File the names, addresses, and phone numbers of key people at each graduate school to which you apply — such people as deans, admissions personnel, financial aid officers, faculty members you have been in contact with, alumni, or anyone else who can be helpful to you.
2. File copies of your written requests for your transcripts to be sent to graduate schools, and record evidence that the transcripts have been received.

3. File your correspondence with faculty members or others who are writing recommendations for you, noting the dates of your requests and evidence that recommendations have been received by the graduate schools.

WARNINGS

A few words to the wise sometimes appear in application instructions, to wit:

"The Admissions Committee urges you to . . . exercise care in completing application forms. The information and statements that you submit to the committee are important factors in the admission decision." — NYU Graduate School of Business Administration

"Incomplete applications cannot be considered. Make sure that you have submitted all required items and completed all forms. You are responsible for ensuring that your application is complete." — Boston University School of Management

"NO APPLICATION to this law school will be processed unless accompanied by a Law School Application Matching Form, which is found in each applicant's LSAT/LSDS registration packet. Since an LSAT and/or LSDS report cannot be produced by the Educational Testing Service without this Matching Form, it will be necessary to return to the applicant any application received without it." — Georgetown University Law Center

---

HOW APPLICATION FORMS MAY DIFFER

You will probably be applying to several graduate programs, in which case you must take care to notice when there are differences in applications, despite their common characteristics. Some applications have their own distinct components, so you must be thoughtful in your responses, and not become inattentive from the boredom of completing a number of them.

But note this important exception: Some but not all medical schools use a common service to administer applications, so that you can apply to several institutions by filing one application with the American Medical College Application Service (AMCAS). The list of medical schools subscribing to the service in forty-one states, Puerto Rico, and the District of Columbia is usually included in the application material of the subscribers.

If you remember the need to tailor each application to its specific requirements, you will then be prepared to spend the necessary time it will take to complete each one. Treat the application process as you would a course assignment; familiarize yourself with each application before starting to fill it out. (This will additionally give you an idea of how much time it is going to take to complete a particular application. Knowing that you may have to spend several hours just responding to one essay question, you will logically then budget your time accordingly.) As you read through an application, pay particular attention to the wording of each request.

Here are some examples of how applications differ:

LENGTH OF ESSAY QUESTIONS

Some graduate schools put no limit on the length of essay question responses, but others ask you to observe a limit on the number of words you write.

- Berkeley's MBA application calls for five essays of specific brevity, between 250 and 500 words.
- Harvard's School of Public Health asks you to confine your two personal statements to a single page of the application, but Johns Hopkins School of Hygiene and Public Health does not limit the personal statement to the single sheet provided with the application.
- Vanderbilt's Owen School of Management puts no limit on the candidate's answer to this request: "Describe the thinking process that led to your decision to study for an MBA and list the factors that most influenced that process, both positive and negative."
- Duke Fuqua School of Business and the School of Law are very insistent that the personal statement not exceed 600 words: "Applicants will disadvantage themselves by disregarding this limit," is the warning on the application.

It is usually harder to be brief and succinct, so plan accordingly when asked for few words. Do not exceed the limit cited.

UNUSUAL REQUESTS

Some applications call for evidence of a candidate's qualifications. Berkeley's MBA candidates are asked to show proficiency in mathematics. Virginia residents applying to any graduate program at the University of Virginia must include with their application for admission an Application for In-State Tuition Rates. Cornell Law School applicants are told: "The most helpful letters of recommendation are those that provide detailed comments about your academic abilities, compared with those of other students applying to law schools." Additional letters of recommendation may be submitted, "but you should recognize that the law of diminishing returns applies here, as elsewhere."

THE SURPRISE ESSAY QUESTION

The following question is posed to NYU's MBA candidates:

"Many jobs will require you to move to various locations within the United

States and throughout the world. Imagine that you have just been transferred to a remote city that has very little to offer in the way of cultural activities or entertainment and you will have to fill your nonworking hours with activities of your own creation. What would you choose to take with you and what would you do to occupy your leisure time? (You may not choose to work extra hours.)"

The answer requires thought and honesty. It would not be sensible to say that you would teach yourself to play a musical instrument in this case if you have never done anything like this before. On the other hand, to say that you would complete a home course in Spanish which you have not had time to finish would be convincing and impressive.

A VARYING NUMBER OF APPLICATION ITEMS

Dartmouth Medical School applicants are urged in a full page of instructions to keep a record of the various steps they must take — including special procedures for early admissions and on-campus interviews. This is good advice to applicants applying to any graduate program, as it is a way to keep track of what you have done and must do. Applying to the University of Virginia Law School, as another example, requires that seven distinct items be mailed, including test scores, transcripts, references, and a Dean's Certification Form from any or all of the undergraduate institutions attended by the applicant.

MED SCHOOLS LOOK FOR CLEAR WRITING, NOT CREATIVE WRITING

Medical school applicants often worry needlessly about their limited writing abilities. Most of them concentrate in one science or another, and such courses and lab work do not require the refined writing expected in liberal arts courses. Medical school admissions committees realize this and therefore, unlike other admissions committees, do not look for creativity or imagination in candidates' writing. What is expected is an ability to write clearly, and most candidates with a strong science background are used to writing clear descriptions, analyses, and solutions to scientific problems.

If you believe you qualify for medical school, your admission will depend on your academic record, your MCAT scores, and the recommendations of your science professors. Where the application calls for a personal statement, you need only write what you have to say in a matter-of-fact style, without trying to be literary or verbose. Pay attention to grammar and spelling, of course, by proofreading. This will show that you are a careful writer who takes pains to be correct.

We cite the above distinctions in order to encourage you to devote your utmost attention to applications for graduate programs. Remember, your application should reflect your maturity, your willingness to make that extra effort to double-check everything and to avoid careless admissions and careless mistakes. Make each application as clear and easy to read as possible. In this way you are letting admissions committees know that you are very serious about your candidacy.

HOW MANY APPLICATIONS SHOULD YOU FILE?

When we hear of a good student applying to twenty medical schools, we shudder. Each application costs $20 to $75. This kind of overkill is not only wasteful of money, it is not practical. The student we have in mind quickly was admitted to eight of the best medical schools in the country, and she got into most of the others she'd applied to also.

It is true that no one can guarantee anyone admission to a medical school. The competition is simply too severe. But those who are likely to be admitted will not improve their chances by ranging all over the place with applications. And if certain students feel that they are marginal applicants, a few applications to the least prestigious medical schools are adequate. Rejection by such schools means medicine is not for them, and they can then regroup and consider public health or some other profession.

In the case of applying to other graduate programs, the formula followed in applying to college still holds. You pick programs that seem to be appropriate to your capacity.

Eric Deloon, a Dutch student, was seeking an American business education. He was just an average college student, yet he applied to Dartmouth, Cornell, Duke, Vanderbilt, and Babson, all of which turned him down. On the advice of the Educational Consulting Center, he then applied to nine hospital management programs: George Washington University, University of Miami, Northwestern, Tulane, University of Michigan, Cornell, Washington University, NYU, and the University of North Carolina. He was admitted to Tulane, George Washington, Washington University, and NYU.

This is not to say that nine is either the limit on places to apply or the average. You apply to the best graduate schools among those where you believe you have a chance of admission. Deloon had a chance at the five programs that rejected him, but he didn't make it. These were not simply wasted applications; they were necessary to bolster his general chance of admission.

REMEMBER TO BUDGET BOTH MONEY AND TIME

Graduate program application fees run from $20 to $75 each, but there are other costs — postage, long-distance phone calls, visits to institutions, photocopying, possibly typing charges if you aren't sure of your typing. Budgeting several hundred dollars to pay for the entire application process makes sense. If you anticipate this necessary layout of funds, you will not be unpleasantly and inconveniently surprised in the middle of preparing applications to find yourself short of money for fees.

How much time has to be devoted to the application process? More than you probably imagine. You should allow yourself time to:

- peruse catalogues and program brochures;
- narrow your choice of programs to a dozen or less;
- study each application form and its instructions;
- complete applications;
- line up your references so they will be prepared to respond in a timely fashion;
- visit institutions if need be;
- be interviewed if an interview is required.

All this must be done with an eye to the time limit imposed by application deadlines and by the constant drumbeat from admissions committees to APPLY EARLY. And remember that while you are doing all this, you must also be carrying on your academic or professional life.

The application process can be vexing, because it often seems so routine. Try to treat it as a challenge and a test of your patience and attention to detail.

THE QUESTION OF INTERVIEWS

There are several points to be made about interviews: (1) Not all graduate program admissions committees require them. (2) Those that do rarely reject a candidate on the basis of an interview. (3) Some do not even grant them if requested. (4) Some candidates eagerly seek them, while other candidates are uneasy about them.

Our advice is this: If interviews are optional and you dread them, then exercise your option and avoid them. Those who, on the other hand, eagerly seek interviews should not expect that they can talk their way into admission. Such candidates often have some weakness in their record that they seek to overcome through persuasiveness and charm. This rarely works.

Those who are uneasy about interviews and are requested to make an appointment for one should realize that it is quite natural to feel a little nervous, since an interview comes down to a personal evaluation of you by a stranger. It is a mistake, however, to try to quell your nervousness through a deliberate effort to make an impression. It is best to be your natural self. Reveal as much about yourself as an interviewer seeks to find out. If you're the quiet type, let that be your manner. If you're ebullient, don't try to suppress it.

You should avoid flattering the interviewer, since this will be perceived as obsequiousness, as apple polishing. Personal remarks are always risky. "I see you are a Phi Bete. So am I," is not just idle chatter, it's an effort to put yourself on the same level as the interviewer, who may be a potential Nobel laureate — or thinks of himself in such terms. Furthermore, the record of your academic prowess is already known to the admissions committee, so there is no need to boast about it.

Remember that the interviewer has interviewed many, many candidates and will certainly be a shrewd judge of character, on to all the tricks of deception that failed candidates have tried. The self-assurance of an interviewer can sometimes be unsettling and tempt you to aggressiveness, even hostility. Avoid the temptation. You are the guest, you are the supplicant, and you are competing with a lot of very cool applicants who do not let anything get under their skins.

There is this distinction between undergraduate and graduate school interviews: For a graduate school interview you should arrive with an agenda. An experienced counselor advises her applicants to graduate school, "Be prepared to answer the question: 'Why are you here?' " Agenda items can run from questions you still have about the program, to questions about the faculty, to a discussion of the issue of sexism or racism at a particular institution, or a discussion of the life of spouses at a graduate school.

Some admissions offices and committees do not have the staff to conduct as many interviews as are requested. Much as you might like to personalize your application and possibly influence a decision in your favor by what you say in an interview, you may have to forgo it and, like most of the other candidates, take your chances on your record and what you have said about yourself on the application.

In any case interviews have not always proved to be helpful in making admissions decisions, because they are brief and therefore can produce only limited impressions. Nonetheless, you should never make the mistake of not taking an interview seriously. Yours is a serious mission: to undertake graduate work. What you have to say in an interview should be relevant and serious.

Medical school interviews are a special case. When a medical school asks a candidate in for an interview, it means that his or her transcript, test scores, and application reveal a potential medical school student. The interview will be evaluative. You will be one of several candidates being interviewed. Such an interview can make the difference between acceptance and rejection. This certainly is enough to make anyone nervous, but the same advice as found above applies: Don't put on an act; be yourself. It's you the school is interested in, not some artificial person you may become if you don't act naturally.

There are some graduate programs that require an interview, but this is less an evaluative interview than an informative one. The committee wants to make sure that applicants understand what the program is all about before they apply.

You should dress well for an interview. Jeans are inappropriate. Women should wear skirts, men should wear sport jackets or a suit, a clean shirt, and a necktie.

The cardinal sin, again, is artificiality, putting on an act in an interview. The only mistake you can make is to worry too much about the impression you are making. It is natural to be a bit tense and cautious with a stranger. But remember that in most cases the chance that you will affect the admissions committee decision one way or the other in an interview is very small.

VISITS TO GRADUATE SCHOOLS ARE OPTIONAL

Other things being equal it would be useful to visit the graduate schools to which you are applying, but it probably just isn't as practical to plan a number of trips to institutions as it was when you were in high school. If you are finishing your college career, you won't have much time, and if you are working, you won't have the freedom in all likelihood.

Still, graduate schools do welcome visits, and will show you around and answer your questions, without necessarily granting an evaluative interview. You can probably arrange to meet one or two faculty members, and you can sit in on a class or two, chat with students, and make your own observations about whether you should apply to this place or that.

The campus visit may be more useful to minorities and women than to others. For them it is all important that the institution where they do their graduate work respond positively to their needs and interests. Talking to students and faculty will bring out the positive and negative aspects of pursuing a graduate program at a particular university. A visit may also be useful if you have a spouse who needs work and wonders what jobs will be available at the school or in the community. In these cases a campus visit or two may be worth the extra effort and cost. It is better to avoid the wrong school than to enroll and then feel you have to drop out or transfer.

What is certain, though, is that visiting graduate schools is not required (except rarely, for interviews) and certainly can have no possible bearing on admission decisions. It can affect your own choice of school, and, providing you are admitted, the visit will have proved profitable.

THE NITTY-GRITTY OF THE APPLICATION PROCESS

Assuming that you have submitted perfect applications to half a dozen graduate programs, now what? Do you just wait for responses and worry, or do you have a rational plan that tells you, for example, when to expect to hear from each institution? It will make a difference to your peace of mind if you keep track of certain things like the probable response date, and also whether the institution has received your transcript, test scores, and recommendations.

It's easy enough to keep a file of photocopies of all your applications, each with the following checklist clipped to the top:

Date mailed......................
Date response expected ....
Date of actual response.............
Transcript acknowledged ....
Test scores acknowledged...........
Recommendations acknowledged ....
Letter of acceptance sent ....
Letter of regret sent...............
Action taken if admitted:
Deposit sent in ....
Faculty contacts made if necessary ...

How do you get the necessary information? When in doubt call the office of the admissions committee and ask someone to check your file. You generally know when to expect a response from instructions in the application package. Should something happen to transcripts, test scores, or recommendations, the committee will let you know and ask for a resubmission. But for your own satisfaction, you may check with admissions personnel without thinking that you are bothering someone.

You may also use your application file to keep track of financial aid requests, the subject of Step Nine.

ACCEPTANCES MEAN CHOICES

If you have taken the Ten Essential Steps to graduate school admission, the chances are very good that you will be admitted to two or more of the programs to which you have applied. This will be both a euphoric and critical moment; you have reached your penultimate objective: admission. Now you must choose one program in which to enroll. This choice should be made with the same exacting care that you have taken during the entire admissions process. To help you reach a decision in an orderly, detached way, go back to Step One and look at the Graduate School Questionnaire that you filled out. Review the first six questions, which were:

1. Why are you considering graduate school at this time and what are your eventual goals?
2. What are the key characteristics you hope to find in a graduate school?
3. Are there any schools or programs you have an interest in at this time?
4. How important to you is location and size in selecting an institution?
5. Will you need financial aid?
6. Do you wish to work and study part-time?

Given that time has passed since you completed your answers, consider whether you would still answer each question the same way, or have you encountered circumstances that might change your mind? We suggest that you make any corrections necessary, and then make up a short table as follows:

Programs Admitted To:

| Program 1 | Program 2 | Program 3 | (Etc.) |

1. Goals
2. Desired characteristics
3. Prior interest
4. Size and location
5. Financial aid
6. Work

Rate each school in terms of your responses to each question, on a scale of 1 to 10, 10 being best. Adding up the scores will show you how far each graduate school goes to satisfy you. However, you may instinctively disagree with this finding, because you have given the same weight to each criterion, which may not reflect your mindset.

To take an obvious example, say a key characteristic you are looking for in a graduate program is the prestige factor — you would like to enroll in what you believe is thought to be one of the top programs of its kind. This answer, reported in Question 2, may outweigh in importance your answer to Question 4, which may suggest that you want to enroll in a small program in a small community — like Hanover, New Hampshire. Now, you have been admitted to the medical programs of Johns Hopkins, Boston University, the University of Rochester, and Dartmouth.

You, according to the table, narrow your choice to Johns Hopkins or Dartmouth. Hopkins, you feel, has a slight prestige edge over Dartmouth, but it is located in Baltimore. How do you determine the relative importance of the two questions? This is a matter of your own choice. Dartmouth may be the perfect size school for you in the perfect small town. But Hopkins may have some special academic allure. And being in a city, it may offer more clinical opportunities, a chance at working with more poverty patients, for example. In the end you decide to give a greater weight to Question 2, feeling that the key characteristic you have chosen to pursue in a program, prestige, outweighs location and size of the institution. Allowing for this weight in your evaluation of all four programs will change the scores and give you another picture to contemplate.

You can do this sort of comparison with any kind of graduate program, professional or academic. And when you have completed this rational, coldly numerical calculation, you may still hesitate to make your final choice until you have talked to a number of people — undergraduate and graduate faculty members you know, alumni of the programs, your family, your boyfriend, girlfriend, or spouse, your banker if financial aid is a factor in your upcoming decision.

A GOOD TIME TO VISIT GRADUATE PROGRAMS

An option at decision time is to plan a visit to graduate programs you are considering, even if you have already made a visit. What happens during a visit after being admitted but before enrolling can tip the scales toward a decision for or against a program. In the case of the potential medical school student, a visit to Dartmouth may overwhelm him or her because of a love of the outdoors and of skiing (though the time for that in medical school is limited). Or a meeting with students at Johns Hopkins may be so exciting that the student chooses to enroll at Hopkins.

A visit can reveal new things, such as the departure from the program of a professor you expected to work with, a university budget cut that affects your program, or the disappearance from the community of a large corporation that reduces chances of work for your spouse. Conversely, a visit can offer pleasant surprises, such as an invitation to join a special group of graduate students going abroad for a term, an improvement in housing facilities you would occupy, the inauguration of a new series of cultural programs on a rural campus that make it a more exciting place to be.

DECIDING AMONG OFFERS OF ADMISSION

There are two things in particular to observe about this final process of accepting one of several offers of admission:

1. Reason and emotion play roles that are different for each applicant.
2. Your decision should in the end be your own; don't make your decision immediately after listening to a persuasive, powerful personality, for nobody can know you, and what is right for you, as well as you can.

Finally, when you have made your decision, let all the graduate programs that have been good enough to accept you know where you plan to enroll. This is simply a matter of politeness. Most admissions committees expect that many of those accepted will go elsewhere. They have no animus against someone who turns down their institution, but they do like a response to their cordial invitation.

And remember to follow instructions about deposits you are obligated to make before you enroll in a program. This is your earnest money, evidence that you are making a commitment to a new and exciting adventure in your life.

ABOUT REJECTION

We have mentioned the Harvard-or-nowhere syndrome, the emotional attitude that says, "If I can't go to Harvard Law School, I won't go to any law school." If you are tempted to adopt this attitude, certainly your peers won't object. Someone else will gladly take your place at any of the law schools you can get into but do not apply to. We, however, feel an obligation to point out that you may regret such a decision someday, and that you ought to keep your options open by applying elsewhere just in case. Attachment to an institution is admirable, but when the institution is not attached to you, why spurn all other institutions? There are so many good graduate programs in this country in every profession, in all fields, that to cut yourself off from almost all of them because you treasure one is a pity. So get a second opinion. This is one instance when absolute self-reliance is not a good policy.

Of course you can always reapply to your favorite program. Many graduate students have been successful in doing so. But to have hope of being accepted on a second go-round you ought to be able to show something new to the committee that rejected you, as proof that you now belong in their program. This can be some course in which you have done well, some achievement at work, something you have written, an improved test score. It can also happen that fewer candidates will apply this time, so the competition will let up a bit.

Step Ten Checklist

1. Study application instructions for each graduate program to which you are applying, taking particular note of deadlines.
2. Read the application through before filling it in.
3. Be careful to limit essay question responses to the specific lengths requested.
4. Proofread everything you have written. Do not turn in a messy application. Use a typewriter when required to do so.
5. Be sure to sign applications and enclose required fees.
6. Keep a file that records dates of submissions of transcripts, test scores, and recommendations to each place you apply. Be sure to keep the name, address, and phone number of the admissions officer or dean of each place where you apply.
7. Keep a file of correspondence with faculty who are writing recommendations, noting each program to which they are to be sent, and evidence that the recommendations have been received.

Postscript:
Within Graduate Walls

You have enrolled in a good graduate program and are now gathered with your classmates to hear a welcoming address. The following lines are taken from what Director of Admissions Stephen Christakos told the class of 1990 at the Wharton School of Business Administration. It is typical of the encouragement you will get when you begin your graduate education.

Today, I have been asked to speak to you regarding who you are and why you are here. This is an awesome agenda, but I will try to be brief.

The first hurdle at Wharton is to get in. We are expecting to welcome 750 of you here today, the largest class ever to enter Wharton. Despite attempts by the press to suggest otherwise, it was a record year in admissions. When you consider the applicants for our final January entering class, there were *nearly 6,200* people applying for a place at Wharton this past year, including a *record 5,621* applying for one of *your* places today. In the past three years, applications to Wharton have increased 61 percent, the largest increase among top-tier MBA programs. This means that selection has become continually tougher. One of you, in a special note to the admissions committee, commented on the selectivity here by writing, and I quote, "I have read that Wharton can enroll only one applicant in eight. Will it help my chances if I apply with seven dumb friends?"

I have done some quick homework on you, both individually and collectively. One thing is clear, you *are* an impressive group. As happy survivors of Saturday mornings at chilly test centers and Friday nights pounding out essays on your IBM-compatible machines — allow me a few moments to tell you about yourselves:

- You performed well as undergraduates, with a class grade-point average of nearly 3.4.
- Collectively you scored higher than 95 percent of the people who take the GMAT. This is particularly noteworthy since it comes at a time when Wharton is placing greater emphasis on the qualitative criteria

(versus the often more easily measured academic criteria) in admissions. For example, our staff conducted nearly 2,200 personal, evaluative interviews of applicants this past year. It has been a reunion, of sorts, seeing many of you on the sidewalks and in the hallways this past week.

- That some of you are male and some female *SHOULD* be obvious and *that* will *not* be covered in this orientation. That 27 percent of you are women is indication that we have come a long way since Wharton was founded to "attract young MEN of inherited intellect, means, and refinement."
- You are international. Twenty-one percent of you are foreign citizens. Last year, with the School's reputation expanding, Wharton received applications from candidates representing a record *94 countries.*
- We are pleased to be welcoming today 12 percent of you who are members of minority groups. This fall more minority students will enroll in our two MBA classes than ever before.
- One of you is 20, another of you is 43 — and the rest of you are in between! The average age of our classes has been creeping upward; it stands at 26.5 for your class.
- I have heard it said that "a little experience often upsets a lot of theory." Ninety-nine percent of you arrive at Wharton with prior full-time work experience. On average you bring just shy of four years of real-world perspective to our classrooms.
- Far more so than Joseph Wharton (who never went to college), your educational backgrounds are varied. You represent more than 200 undergraduate schools: While about 160 of you attended Ivy League institutions, the Big Ten of the Midwest are not forgotten. There are Hoosiers, Wildcats, and Buckeyes among you. From the West it was interesting to note that there are, I believe, 21 Stanford graduates. And will *BOTH* of our *Texas A and M* alumni meet each other outside of Annenberg after this orientation?
- Upon reviewing your statements of intended major, we observed a dramatic shift with your class this past year. For the first time ever at Wharton, our management department has surpassed finance as the top intended major among you. Popular offerings in entrepreneurial and multinational management have attracted 31 percent of you to our management department. Twenty-seven percent plan to pursue finance, with our marketing department's popularity rising fast (the creative/behaviorist types among you represent 16 percent of your class). For some reason, you are evidently less concerned with getting from one place to another — only a handful of you professed an interest in our transportation major.

It is clear that you are achievers. You wrote with modest and occasional whimsical zeal about your accomplishments. Well, that is, *most* of you wrote with modest zeal. Among what must be a record number of envelopes received from overnight carriers, we received this foam packed, photo-typeset package. The applicant worked in advertising, as you might suspect, and it certainly caught our attention, along with four additional boxes from him which subsequently followed with more goodies. Oh, are you interested in whether he was admitted? Well . . . *NO.* Tell your friends that a *simple* envelope usually suffices!

Speaking of achievements, sitting among you is someone who came to the U.S. through a Vietnamese refugee camp in San Diego; another of you survived the embarrassment of interviewing with us in shorts and a T-shirt after Greyhound lost your clothes. There is also someone who skated for the U.S. National Figure Skating Team, another of you won a National Guild piano award for your concert in Carnegie Hall, there are a Fulbright award winner and two Rhodes semifinalists. One of you was honored by *Time* magazine as one of the United States' top twenty college juniors. Finally, one of you noted as her most significant achievement "having completed essays 2 and 3." And yes, it is absolutely true — in the second-year class there are not one but *two* former contestants on "Wheel of Fortune"!

Your work backgrounds are diverse, and we have been particularly delighted this year with the great number of you who have had significant international experience. Of course, there are healthy portions of commercial and investment bankers among you, consultants, Big 8 accountants, and a few recent, display-setting sales trainees. But here is just a sampling of the former jobs you've held:

- One of you was controller for a Hallmark Greeting Card production facility in Kansas, while another classmate was marketing manager for a cheese company in Mexico.
- One of you produced IBM's award-winning TV commercials, and another of you was a reporter in Washington for the *Nightly Business Report.*
- One of you worked as a professional magician on a cruise ship; another of you was a researcher in the British Treasury for a member of Parliament.
- One of you worked as a jackaroo on a sheep farm in Australia, and another of you was a financial analyst for Chiquita Banana in Costa Rica.
- We have a former dancer for Tokyo's Disneyland, as well as a sweater designer with J. Crew.
- One of you was an international trade lawyer for Toyota Motor Corp., and yet another of you was an Assistant Marketing Director for the National Hockey League.
- There are a number of successful entrepreneurs — one of you started a plastics company that manufactures credit cards; another of you ran a successful diamond-cutting business in Israel. And we chuckled at the one of you who recounted your experience at age five of selling rocks door-to-door.

Your diverse backgrounds are also reflected in your outside interests. There are singers, athletes, and writers among you *and:*

- One of you was a bass player for a rock group called Urban Dogs; another of you was lead singer for The Vegetables.
- One of you was a member of the Kuwait Olympic basketball team; another of you is a candidate for the U.S. Olympic yachting team.
- One of you played harp professionally in the Lincoln Center, while one of you was once the University of Wisconsin mascot, *Bucky Badger!*
- Among you we have a former defensive tackle with the *Japanese* collegiate football champions, and another who holds Philippine power-lifting records.
- We have an importer of aboriginal art, and probably my personal favorite is the producer of a film about a Hungarian immigrant who plays the New York lotto by counting daily the number of dead roaches in his roach motels!

Throughout our evaluation process, it was nice to see that a good number of you know how to market yourselves. You have mastered the cantankerous copy of application forms and permitted yourselves to shine through.

From one of you who worked at a school in California for children who are wards of the court, to another who did missionary work with Mother Teresa, to yet another classmate of yours who helped start a Korean orphanage while stationed there — we've seen plenty of evidence of the very personal, caring and human dimensions to your class.

To close, I want to extend a warm welcome to you on behalf of our 60,000 alumni and 63 Alumni Association Clubs from around the world. After what I know will be two challenging, stimulating, and fun years for you here, you'll be joining an impressive and loyal network of Wharton alumni.

Appendix A:
The Way of Eight Recent
Wesleyan Graduates

The following eight cases have been summarized by the Wesleyan University Career Planning Center, as examples of the varied experiences of good students who have graduated from a highly selective college and gone on to seek further education. They are typical not only of Wesleyan students but of many students who were academically strong in college and active outside the classroom. They are certainly success stories, but they also shed light on the nature of the competition applicants to the better graduate programs face today.

CASE 1

Carolyn, a history major, was very active in campus politics. After writing some stories for the campus newspaper, she competed for and got an internship with a Hartford newspaper. Senior year she began thinking about law school as well as journalism.

After graduation she worked briefly for a Boston newspaper and then was awarded a CORO fellowship which provided a nine-month internship in public service in San Francisco.

She then applied to joint law and journalism programs at Columbia, Northwestern, and Boston University. A year after graduation, Carolyn enrolled at Northwestern.

CASE 2

Lillian majored in government and was active in sports. She considered government, business, and law as career options. During junior year she worked as a volunteer for her state congresswoman. In the summer before senior year, she was an intern in New York City with the Financial Women's Association, and this introduced her to some challenging projects at J. P. Morgan.

Her senior thesis was in government and politics. Interviews resulted in offers from several banks. Lillian then spent two years in a six-person training program with a small trust bank in Boston.

Following this she got an MBA at Kellogg Business School of Northwestern University. She is now in the marketing department of a major New York City bank.

CASE 3

Porter majored in English and did considerable writing, research, and analysis. In college he tutored local children and taught at St. Paul's Summer School junior year. He joined the Peace Corps after graduation, spending two years in Nepal before he took a job interviewing witnesses for the district attorney's office in Washington, D.C.

A year later Porter entered Georgetown Law School.

CASE 4

Cynthia was a strong chemistry major who was undecided whether to get a Ph.D. or an M.D. Summers she did research for a pharmaceutical company. She was interviewed by hospitals, research labs, consulting firms, and pharmaceutical companies.

Cynthia spent her first year out of college with a health-care consulting firm in New York City, and then did a year of research at Yale. She then enrolled in a joint Ph.D./M.D. program at Johns Hopkins.

CASE 5

Isabel considered teaching, social services, and medicine while majoring in molecular biology and biochemistry. Junior year she went to Ethiopia with Scholars Against World Hunger, vaccinating people and helping to feed many who were near starvation.

After graduation she returned to Africa. Isabel enrolled in Harvard Medical School a year later.

CASE 6

Betsy thought she would like a career in educational administration. In college she majored in science and French, played tennis and other sports, and worked summers as a camp counselor. Her junior year was spent in France.

184 / *Appendix A*

Having worked at Wesleyan as an undergraduate in the Career Planning Center, she continued there full-time for two years after graduation as an intern/counselor. She then spent a year in sales for a national HMO (health maintenance organization). Finally, Betsy enrolled in the Yale School of Organization and Management.

CASE 7

Jeffrey's interest in government and international relations led him into a considerable amount of research work with a Wesleyan professor outside of class. Summers he taught at Choate-Rosemary Hall Summer School.

After graduating, Jeffrey spent six months with the Department of Energy in Washington as an intern, and then a semester at the London School of Economics studying political theory. During his first six months after graduation, he was a Carnegie Fellow.

Finally, at the end of his first year out of college, he enrolled in Princeton's Woodrow Wilson School of Politics and International Affairs.

CASE 8

Nora, majoring in sociology, started a counseling service for Hispanic pregnant mothers in a nearby community. During her college years, she was active in an anti-apartheid movement. To help finance her education, she worked for the Wesleyan campus food services all four years and during summers.

While still a senior, Nora was accepted by Smith College's School of Social Work. She expects to make a career in social work.

Appendix B:
Letters of Recommendation

Those applying to graduate school are often required by admissions committees to have letters of recommendation submitted by people who know them well. Such letters carry considerable weight. Most, of course, are confidential, but occasionally, after a candidate is admitted, copies of the letters are sent to the candidate by those who wrote them. The examples here are letters written by a banker and an attorney on behalf of Martin Burdick, whose case was discussed in Step Six. They may serve as models for candidates in suggesting what they should ask for of those who write their recommendations.

To Whom It May Concern

I am writing this letter to recommend Martin Burdick, whom I believe to be an excellent candidate for admission to your business school.

I have known the Burdicks for many years. Martin's father is the current president of Burdick Hardware, Inc., a closely held firm that has done business in New York for over 75 years. The company has grown from a small local enterprise to its present position as a strong and important member of the New York business community.

The challenge of managing a company such as Burdick is major. The company is in an intensely competitive industry, functioning on several levels of distribution and retailing. Burdick has had the good fortune of being directed by a sophisticated second generation of management and has emerged in very good position for long-term continued growth if it can expand its managerial content. This is the crucial problem facing many companies of Burdick's size.

Martin is an ideal candidate for an MBA degree in that he has the interest and ability to succeed at graduate school, and the strong opportunity to put that experience to good use early on.

This past summer I had the opportunity to work with Martin on a sizable venture — a recent acquisition by Burdick which my bank helped finance.

You can rest assured that he is serious, intelligent, and would be a valuable contributor to your program.

Sincerely

Dear ——

This is written in support of Mr. Martin Burdick's application for admission to your Master of Business Administration Program.

In the course of my present professional activities as an attorney I have, in the past two years, had occasion to deal with Mr. Burdick in two separate merger negotiations. Both of these matters involved serious business and interpersonal problems.

Throughout the course of these negotiations I had reason to observe, and was very much impressed by, Mr. Burdick's performance under pressure as an important member of one of the negotiating teams. In both of these negotiations, and under different circumstances (one of the negotiations ended in a successful buyout and the other did not), Mr. Burdick exhibited in-depth business knowledge, poise, and especially an understanding of interpersonal nuances to an extent not ordinarily found in so young a man.

I have in the past had occasion to observe closely many young businessmen in various stages of their careers. Based on that experience and my observations of Mr. Burdick, I can strongly recommend him as a candidate for your Master of Business Administration program, in the full belief that he would both benefit from and contribute to that program.

Very truly yours

Bibliography

Business and Management Education

Guide to Graduate Management Education, Charlotte Kurst, Editor. Princeton, NJ: The Graduate Management Admission Council, 1982.

Inside Management Training: The Career Guide to Management Training Programs for College Graduates, Marian L. Salzman and Deidre Sullivan. New York: New American Library, 1985.

The Insider's Guide to the Top Ten Business Schools, Tom Fischgrund, Editor. 3rd ed. Boston: Little, Brown and Company, 1988.

The Managers: Career Alternatives for the College Educated, Richard Thain. Bethesda, MD: College Placement Council, Inc., 1978.

National Center for Service-Learning Action (NCSLA), 806 Constitution Avenue NW, Room 1106, Washington, DC 20525; (800) 425-8580. Government Clearing House for Service Learning Opportunity.

National Society for Internships and Experienced Education (NSIEE), 810 18th St. NW, Suite 307, Washington, DC 20006; (202) 331-1516. Nonprofit organization. Offers newsletter, peer assistance network, internship directories.

1986 Internships: 34,000 On-The-Job Training Opportunities for All Types of Careers, Lisa S. Hulse, Editor. Garrett Park, MD: Garrett Park Press, 1989.

Occupational Outlook Handbook, Annual, Neal H. Rosenthal, Editor. Washington, DC: Bureau of Labor Statistics, Superintendent of Documents, U.S. Government Printing Office.

The Official Guide to MBA: Programs, Admissions, and Careers, Charlotte Kurst, Editor. Princeton, NJ: Graduate Management Admissions Council, 1988.

Standard & Poor's Register of Corporations, Directors and Executives, Annual, 3 vols. New York: Standard & Poor's Corp.

Toughing It Out at Harvard: The Making of a Woman MBA, Fran Warden Henry. New York: G. P. Putnam's Sons, 1983.

Career Planning and Decision-Making

Bibliography of Careers in International Affairs. New York: The United Nations Association of the U.S.A., New York: 1980.

The Career Finder: Pathways to Over 1,500 Jobs for the Future, Lester Schwartz and Irv Brechner. New York: Ballantine Books, 1983.

Career Placement Council Annual. Bethlehem, PA: Career Placement Council, 1988.

Careers in International Affairs, Gerald Sheehan, Editor. Washington, DC: School of Foreign Service, Georgetown University, 1982.

Careers in the Military: Good Training for Civilian Life, Robert Rafferty. New York: E.P. Dutton, 1980.

College to Career: The Guide to Job Opportunities, Joyce Slayton Mitchell. New York: College Entrance Examination Board, 1986.

The Harvard Guide to Careers, Martha P. Leape. Cambridge, MA: Harvard University Press, 1983.

Harvard Guide to Careers in Communications, Laurie Stauffer. Cambridge, MA: Harvard University Press, 1980.

How to Choose, Change, Advance Your Career, Adele Lewis, William Lewis, and Steven Radlauer. Hauppage, NY: Barron's Educational Series, Inc., 1983.

International Jobs: Where They Are and How to Get Them, Eric Kocher. Reading, MA: Addison-Wesley, 1984.

Invest Yourself: A Catalogue of Volunteer Opportunities, Susan Angus, Editor. New York: Commission on Voluntary Service and Action, 1983.

Jobs for English Majors and Other Smart People, John L. Munschauer. Princeton, NJ: Peterson's Guides, Inc., 1982.

Money Jobs: Training Programs Run by Banking, Accounting, Insurance, and Brokerage Firms — and How to Get into Them, Marti Prashker and S. Peter Valiunas. New York: Crown Publishers, 1985.

Engineering and Physical Sciences

Engineering Education: Engineering College Research and Graduate Study, Annual. Washington, DC: American Society for Engineering Education.

The Engineering/High Tech Students' Handbook: Preparing for Careers of the Future, David Reyes-Guerra and Alan Fischer. Princeton, NJ: Peterson's Guides, 1987.

Graduate Programs and Admissions Manual, 1987-88, Volume C: *Physical Sciences, Mathematics, and Engineering.* Princeton, NJ: Educational Testing Service.

Graduate Programs in Physics, Astronomy, and Related Fields, 1984-85, Dion Shea, Editor. 7th ed. New York: American Institute of Physics, 1984.

Peterson's Annual Guides to Graduate Study, Volume 5: *Engineering and Applied Sciences;* Volume 4: *Physical Sciences and Mathematics.* Princeton, NJ: Peterson's Guides, Inc.

Financial Aid Information

Free Money for Professional Studies, Laurie Blum. New York: Barnes & Noble Books, 1985.

Grants for Graduate Studies, 1986-88, Andrea Leskes, Editor. Princeton, NJ: Peterson's Guides, Inc., 1986.

A Guide to Scholarships, Fellowships, and Grants: A Selected Bibliography, Kathleen Slowik and Diane D'Angelo. New York: Institute of International Education, 1988.

The Individual's Guide to Grants, Judith B. Margolin. New York: Plenum Press, 1983.

Graduate Academic Disciplines: Economics, Humanities, Political Science and International Affairs, Life Sciences, Social and Behavioral Sciences

Graduate Programs and Admissions Manual, 1983-84, Volume A: *Agriculture, Biological Sciences, Psychology, Health Sciences, and Humanities.* Princeton, NJ: Educational Testing Service, 1984.

Graduate Programs and Admissions Manual, 1983-84, Volume D: *Social Sciences and Education.* Princeton, NJ: Educational Testing Service, 1984.

Graduate Study in Psychology, 1983-84. Washington, DC: American Psychology Association, 16th ed., 1982.

Guide to American Graduate Schools, Herbert B. Livesey and Harold Doughty. New York: Viking Press, 5th ed., 1986.

Guide to Graduate Study in Economics, Agricultural Economics, and Related Fields, Wyn F. Owen, Editor. Homewood, IL: American Economics Association, 6th ed., 1982.

Guide to Graduate Study in Political Science. Washington, DC: American Political Science Association, 1982.

Higher Education Directory, 1988. Washington, DC: Higher Education Publications, 1988.

Peterson's Guides to Graduate Study, Volume 2: *Humanities and Social Sciences,* Annual. Princeton, NJ: Peterson's Guides, Inc.

Health and Medicine

Allied Health Education Directory. Chicago: American Medical Association, 11th ed., 1982.

Barron's Guide to Financial Aid for Medical Students, Dr. Stephen H. Lazar. Hauppage, NY: Barron's Educational Services, Inc., 1979.

Dentistry: Handbook for Predental Advisors. Chicago: American Predental Advisors, 1987.

Health Services Administration Education, 1987, Marcia S. Lane, Editor, Biennial. Arlington, VA: Association of University Programs in Health Administration.

Medical School Admissions Requirements 1988-89: United States and Canada, Annual. Washington, DC: Association of American Medical Colleges.

Medical School, Getting In/Staying In, Keith Ablov. Baltimore: Williams and Wilkins, 1986.

Peterson's Annual Guides to Graduate Study, Volume 3: Biological, Agricultural, and Health Sciences, Annual. Princeton, NJ: Peterson's Guides, Inc.

Veterinary Medical School Admission Requirements in the United States and Canada, 1988-89, Marcia James Sawyer, Editor. Bethesda, MD: Betz Publishing Co., Inc., 1987.

For the International Student

English Language and Orientation Programs in the United States, Biennial. New York: Institute of International Education.

Financial Planning for Study in the United States. Princeton, NJ: College Entrance Examination Board, 1984.

A Foreign Student's Guide to Financial Assistance for Study and Research in the United States, Joe Lurie, Editor. Garden City, NY: Adelphi University Press, 1983.

Law School and Legal Careers

Barron's Guide to Law Schools, Elliott M. Epstein and Lawrence M. Troy. 8th ed. Hauppage, NY: Barron's Educational Series, Inc., 1988.

Financing Your Law School Education, John R. Kramer, Editor. Newtown, PA: Law School Admission Services/Law School Admission Council, 1986.

Inside the Law Schools, Sally Goldfarb. New York: E. P. Dutton, 1986.

The Prelaw Handbook: The Official Guide to U.S. Law Schools. Newtown, PA: Law School Admission Services/Law School Admission Council, 1987-88.

The Right School for You, Rennard Strickland, Editor. Newtown, PA: Law School Admission Services, 1986.

Testing

Directory of Selected National Testing Programs & Test Collections, compiled by Educational Testing Service Staff. Phoenix, AZ: Onyx Press, 1987.

Index